Dark Psychology & Manipulation Defense

Defend Yourself From Insidious Tactics and Learn to
Recognize Covert Manipulation, Mind Control, and
Unwanted Persuasion Used to Trap Innocent Victims

Timothy John

Table of Contents

Introduction

Have you ever felt an unsettling push toward decisions that didn't quite resonate with your heart? Have your emotions ever been swayed without your permission, or have you sensed someone gently yet persistently pushing at your personal boundaries? If these scenarios sound familiar, you're not alone. Like many others, you may have unwittingly become a part of the subtle yet powerful world of dark psychology. In the shadows of everyday interactions, manipulation, undue influence, and covert control are more common than we might want to believe. Yet, there's a glimmer of hope: By becoming aware of these tactics and understanding them, we can reclaim our freedom to think and choose for ourselves.

This book is a journey into understanding how love and trust can be weaponized, how the subtle art of manipulation can be masked as affection, and how to recognize and resist these underhanded tactics. It's an exploration designed to empower you, help you identify these maneuvers, provide you with strategies to uphold your autonomy, and make decisions that align with your true values and priorities.

Imagine walking through life's interactions equipped with the knowledge to discern when your independence of thought is being challenged. Whether in personal relationships or professional dealings, recognizing the nuances of manipulation can fundamentally alter your engagement with the world. This understanding is key to protecting your mental and emotional well-being.

As you delve into these pages, you're embarking on a path of enlightenment and challenges. You're facing the reality of those who weaponize love and trust by learning to dismantle their strategies. This journey isn't just about identifying manipulative behavior. It's about forging a path where your autonomy and individuality are acknowledged and celebrated.

This book isn't merely a collection of information; it's a guide to personal liberation. It's a call to recognize and break free from the hidden influences in your life. Here, you're not just absorbing information, you're taking an active role in reclaiming your freedom, one conscious decision at a time.

CHAPTER 1:

The World of Dark Psychology

Picture a regular neighborhood gathering, a friendly barbecue hosted by a well-liked couple, Tom and Linda. Guests mingle, enjoying the warm evening, the smell of grilling food, and the sound of laughter. Among the guests is Emily, a recent addition to the neighborhood, who is having a chat with Tom. Emily, a soft-spoken and kind individual, is expressing her concerns about an ongoing community issue.

As they talk, Tom's demeanor is sympathetic, but his words are carefully calculated. He agrees with Emily, feeding her worries, while subtly steering the conversation to undermine another neighbor, whom he subtly portrays as the root cause of many community issues. His skill lies in making his manipulation appear as genuine concern, painting himself as an ally while sowing seeds of discord.

Emily, unaware of Tom's true intentions, finds herself increasingly aligned with his perspective. By the end of the conversation, she feels a mix of gratitude for Tom's *insights* and a newfound wariness toward the other neighbor. Tom's ability to manipulate the narrative and influence Emily's perceptions without overt coercion is a textbook example of dark psychology.

This scenario, unfolding quietly amid a social event, highlights the insidious nature of dark psychology. It's not always about overt domination or control. Often, it's about influencing perceptions, altering realities, and bending wills in a way that goes unnoticed by the victims. It's a subtle dance of influence and manipulation, occurring in the most ordinary settings.

This chapter explores the workings of dark psychology that hide in plain sight. We'll examine the strategies employed by individuals like Tom to manipulate and control, often under the guise of normal social interaction. This exploration will not only make you more aware of such tactics but also equip you with the knowledge to recognize and counteract them in your own life.

What Is Dark Psychology?

Dark psychology is a term that encapsulates the study and application of psychological principles and tactics used for manipulative, coercive, or malicious purposes. At its heart, it represents a side of human psychology that is often shrouded in secrecy and taboo, revolving around the use of influence, persuasion, and manipulation to achieve selfish ends. This field of psychology explores the darker aspects of human behavior, delving into how individuals can use knowledge of psychological principles to exploit, control, or harm others.

This concept extends beyond the simplistic notion of good versus evil; it's about understanding the complexities and nuances of human behavior. Dark psychology encompasses a range of behaviors and tactics, from subtle manipulation to overt acts of deceit and coercion. It is not limited to criminal or antisocial individuals; everyday people can also employ these tactics, often unconsciously.

One of the key elements of dark psychology is the understanding and manipulation of human emotions. Manipulators skilled in dark psychology are adept at reading emotional cues and exploiting them for their gain. They can play on fears, insecurities, desires, and other emotions to influence and control others. This emotional manipulation is often subtle, making it difficult for victims to recognize and defend against.

Another aspect is the strategic use of information and misinformation. In the realm of dark psychology, knowledge is power. By controlling the flow of information, manipulators can create environments of uncertainty and dependency. They can withhold information, distort facts, or feed half-truths to maintain an upper hand in relationships or situations.

Besides emotional manipulation and information control, dark psychology also involves a calculated use of social dynamics. It includes understanding and exploiting social hierarchies, group norms, and relationships. Manipulators may use tactics like peer pressure, social isolation, or the creation of in- and out-groups to exert control over individuals or groups.

Dark psychology is a multifaceted and complex field that explores the use of psychological tactics for manipulation and control. It encompasses emotional manipulation, information control, and social dynamics, with the ultimate goal of power and influence. While it can be used for harmful purposes, an understanding of dark psychology can also serve as a valuable tool for protection and prevention.

Now, let's examine who typically employs these tactics and the different contexts in which dark psychology can be seen.

Who Uses Dark Psychology, and Where Can It Be Used?

Dark psychology has a varied user base that spans different contexts. Contrary to popular belief, the use of these tactics is not confined to individuals with malicious intent or psychopathic tendencies. In reality, we can find dark psychology in everyday interactions, often used by ordinary people.

In politics, for instance, dark psychology is frequently employed. Politicians may use manipulative tactics to sway public opinion, discredit opponents, or rally support for controversial policies. They might leverage fear, appeal to biases, or use charisma to obscure the truth and manipulate the masses. This is clear in political campaigns where misinformation and emotional manipulation are often used to influence voters' perceptions and decisions.

In personal relationships, dark psychology takes on a more intimate and potentially harmful form. It's not just about the obvious abuser or the narcissistic partner; sometimes, it's the subtle manipulator who, under the guise of care and concern, controls and influences their partner. These tactics can range from gaslighting, where a person's reality is distorted, to more overt forms of emotional blackmail.

The workplace is another common setting for these tactics. Office politics can involve manipulative behaviors like backstabbing, rumor-spreading, or taking credit for others' work. Dark psychology here is often about climbing the corporate ladder or maintaining power and control within an organization. Leaders or colleagues may use their influence to undermine others, foster unhealthy competition, or create a culture of dependency and fear.

Moreover, dark psychology finds its place in the media and advertising. Here, manipulation often comes as persuasive advertising techniques designed to exploit consumers' insecurities, desires, and fears. By understanding and tapping into the psychological triggers of their audience, advertisers can influence buying behaviors and shape consumer attitudes.

Despite its widespread use, the motivations behind employing dark psychology vary. Some individuals may use these tactics consciously and deliberately for personal gain, while others might do so unconsciously, as a learned behavior or a defense mechanism. It's crucial to recognize that the use of dark psychology isn't always a clear-cut case of right or wrong; sometimes, it's a complex interplay of individual psychology, social conditioning, and situational dynamics.

We can't limit dark psychology to any specific group or setting, but what leads people to rely on dark psychological tactics, and what motivates them to manipulate and control others? This exploration is crucial to comprehending the full spectrum of dark psychology.

Why Do People Use Dark Psychology?

The motivations behind the use of dark psychology are as varied and complex as human behavior itself. At its most fundamental level, the use of manipulative tactics is often driven by a desire for power, control, or personal gain. However, to truly understand these motivations, we must delve deeper into the human psyche.

One common motivator is insecurity. Individuals who feel insecure about their position, abilities, or relationships may turn to manipulation as a way to assert control and alleviate their insecurities. By controlling others, they create a false sense of security and superiority. For instance, a manager who feels threatened by a competent subordinate might use undermining tactics to maintain their perceived superiority in the workplace.

Another driver is a desire for personal gain or advancement. In competitive environments, whether in business, politics, or social settings, individuals may use dark psychology as a tool to outmaneuver rivals and achieve their goals. This can manifest in various forms, from subtle manipulation to outright deceit and coercion.

Some individuals use dark psychology out of a need for self-preservation. In situations where they feel vulnerable or at risk, manipulation can become a defense mechanism. This is often seen in toxic relationships, where one partner may employ manipulative tactics as a means of maintaining the relationship or protecting themselves from perceived emotional harm.

There are also those who use dark psychology simply because they can. Individuals with narcissistic or sociopathic traits may manipulate others for amusement, to demonstrate their power, or because they lack empathy and don't comprehend the harm they cause. For these individuals, manipulation is not a means to an end, but an end in itself.

However, not all uses of dark psychology are nefarious. In certain professions, such as law enforcement or psychology, understanding and employing aspects of dark psychology can be crucial in dealing with criminal behavior or protecting oneself from manipulation. In these cases, the motivation is to serve the greater good or to protect oneself and others from harm.

The motivations behind the use of dark psychology are diverse, ranging from insecurity and personal gain to self-preservation and, in some cases, malevolence. Understanding these motivations is key to recognizing, countering, and ultimately preventing manipulative behaviors in our lives and the lives of those around us.

Is Dark Psychology Good or Bad?

The moral evaluation of dark psychology is not straightforward. It is neither inherently good nor inherently bad: It exists within a spectrum influenced by intent, context, and consequences. To comprehend its ethical dimensions, it is vital to consider the varied applications and outcomes of these psychological tactics.

In certain contexts, the knowledge and application of dark psychological principles can serve beneficial purposes. For instance, in law enforcement, understanding manipulative tactics can be crucial in interrogating suspects or undercover operations. Similarly, in psychology or counseling, professionals might use their understanding of dark psychology to help clients who have been victims of manipulation, providing them with strategies to recognize and counteract these tactics.

However, more often than not, the use of dark psychology is associated with negative connotations due to its exploitative nature. When used for personal gain at the expense of others, it becomes a tool for harm. This is particularly evident in relationships or interactions where there is an imbalance of power. For example, a leader who uses fear and manipulation to control their team creates a toxic work environment, leading to stress, low morale, and high turnover.

The ethical implications of using dark psychology also depend on the awareness and consent of those involved. Manipulative tactics that exploit, deceive, or coerce others without their knowledge or consent are generally considered unethical. This is because they violate principles of respect, autonomy, and fairness.

However, the morality of using dark psychological tactics can be ambiguous in certain situations. For instance, a person might use subtle manipulation in a negotiation to achieve a fair outcome or to protect themselves from exploitation. In such cases, the ethical nature of the tactics used can be debated based on the intentions behind them and the resulting consequences.

It is also crucial to consider the long-term effects of employing dark psychology. Regular reliance on manipulative tactics can lead to a breakdown in trust and integrity, both in personal and professional relationships. It can foster an environment where deceit, suspicion, and power games become the norm, leading to harmful psychological and social outcomes.

The ethical evaluation of dark psychology is complex and context-dependent. While it can be used for positive purposes, it is more commonly associated with negative outcomes because of its exploitative nature. Understanding the ethical implications of these tactics is essential for making informed decisions about when and how they are used.

Navigating through the ethical complexities of dark psychology brings us to a crucial aspect of its impact: the dangers associated with its misuse. By examining real-life scenarios, we can gain a deeper understanding of how the reckless employment of dark psychological tactics can lead to detrimental consequences for an individual's character and their interpersonal relationships.

The Dangers of Dark Psychology: An Anecdote

Consider Alex, a mid-level manager in a tech company. Alex had always been ambitious, striving to climb the corporate ladder. To achieve his goals, he began employing tactics he had learned from studying dark psychology: subtle manipulation, playing team members against each other, and exploiting their weaknesses for his benefit. Initially, these tactics seemed to work; he gained a reputation as a results-driven manager and even secured a few promotions.

However, the long-term effects of Alex's methods were far from positive. His team, once collaborative and innovative, became riddled with mistrust and internal conflict. The best talents started leaving, unable to thrive in the toxic environment he had created. Colleagues avoided him, and his superiors questioned his leadership abilities.

Alex's personal life was not spared either. His manipulative behavior seeped into his relationships with friends and family, leading to isolation and strained interactions. His friends found him untrustworthy, and family members felt used and unappreciated.

The most significant toll, however, was on Alex himself. Over time, his reliance on dark psychological tactics eroded his sense of self. He became increasingly paranoid, always on edge, fearing that others would use similar tactics against him. His personal and professional relationships suffered, and he found himself alone, both at work and in his personal life.

This anecdote illustrates the inherent dangers of misusing dark psychology. While it may offer short-term gains, the long-term consequences can be devastating. It can lead to damaged relationships, loss of trust, and a compromised moral compass, ultimately isolating the individual from meaningful connections and collaborations.

Having explored the dangers inherent in the misuse of dark psychology, we now turn our attention to the traits commonly exhibited by individuals who employ these tactics. By understanding these characteristics, we can better recognize and protect ourselves from potential manipulation and its harmful effects.

Traits of Dark Psychology Users

Individuals who habitually use dark psychology often exhibit a constellation of traits that can serve as red flags for those around them. Understanding these traits is key to recognizing and responding appropriately to manipulative behavior.

1. **Inflated Sense of Self-Worth:** Many users of dark psychology possess an exaggerated sense of their importance and abilities.

This narcissistic trait leads them to believe they deserve special treatment and may manipulate others for their ends. Their egocentric perspective often blinds them to the needs and rights of others.

2. **Lack of Empathy:** A defining characteristic of frequent manipulators is a diminished capacity for empathy. They struggle to understand or care about the feelings and well-being of others, making it easier for them to exploit and harm without remorse. This lack of empathy is dangerous as it allows them to justify their actions no matter the impact on others.

3. **Moral Disengagement:** Individuals adept in dark psychology often exhibit moral disengagement: a process where they rationalize or justify unethical behavior. By convincing themselves that their actions are acceptable, necessary, or deserved by their victims, they detach themselves from the moral implications of their actions.

4. **Manipulative and Deceitful Behavior:** A propensity for manipulation and deceit is a hallmark of those who use dark psychology. They are skilled at lying, twisting facts, and employing psychological tactics to control or deceive others. This behavior can range from subtle manipulation to outright deceit and coercion.

5. **Charm and Charisma:** Interestingly, many individuals who use dark psychology can be charming and charismatic. They use these traits to attract and disarm others, making it easier to exert influence and control. This charm, however, is often superficial, serving as a mask for more sinister motives.

6. **Strategic and Calculating:** They tend to be strategic and calculating, often planning their actions to maximize their benefit. They are adept at reading situations and people, using this information to manipulate outcomes in their favor.

7. **Exploitation of Power Dynamics:** These individuals are often skilled at exploiting power dynamics, whether in personal relationships, the workplace, or other social settings. They understand how to use their position, or the vulnerabilities of others, to gain an advantage.

Recognizing these traits can be challenging, as individuals who use dark psychology are often adept at hiding their true intentions. However, awareness of these characteristics is the first step in protecting oneself from potential manipulation. It is important to approach interactions with a critical eye, especially when encountering behaviors that align with these traits.

Equipped with an understanding of the traits of dark psychology users, we are better prepared to navigate our interactions with heightened awareness. Our next exploration will delve into the consequences of being unaware of manipulative tactics. Through an illustrative anecdote, we will examine how ignorance of dark psychology can adversely affect an individual's self-esteem, confidence, and overall well-being.

Ignorance Is Not Bliss

Let's follow Jenna, a graphic designer in a small firm. Jenna, known for her talent and dedication, was often praised for her work. However, her manager, Derek, a person who subtly employed dark psychological tactics, saw Jenna's success as a threat to his position. Unbeknownst to Jenna, Derek began using manipulative strategies to undermine her confidence.

He would often give her backhanded compliments, subtly criticize her work in meetings, or take credit for her ideas. He also employed gaslighting tactics, making her question her memory and judgment. For instance, he would deny conversations they had about project directions, leading Jenna to doubt her recollection of events.

Over time, her self-esteem eroded. She started questioning her abilities and feeling less confident in her work. The once-passionate designer found herself feeling anxious and stressed, dreading interactions with Derek. Her performance suffered, affecting her relationships with her colleagues.

Jenna's experience is a stark illustration of the harmful outcomes that can result from being ignorant of manipulative tactics. Derek's dark psychological strategies left her vulnerable to his manipulation.

Therefore, it's important to be aware of and understand dark psychology. Moving from this understanding, we now pivot to the empowering aspect of awareness. By recognizing and understanding the principles of dark psychology, individuals can arm themselves with the knowledge necessary to identify, resist, and counter manipulative behaviors, thus taking control of their interactions and protecting their mental well-being.

Awareness and Empowerment

Understanding and being alert to the tactics of dark psychology is key to protecting our mental and emotional health. This knowledge acts like a shield, helping us spot and stop manipulative actions before they hurt us.

The first step is learning. Knowing about different kinds of manipulation, the signs of psychological abuse, and common dark psychology tactics helps people recognize these actions as they happen. This is especially useful in certain work environments or personal relationships where there's an imbalance of power.

With this knowledge, people can come up with ways to defend themselves against manipulation. This might mean setting firm boundaries, getting advice from friends or professionals, or being more aware of why people do what they do. For instance, understanding what gaslighting is can help someone hold on to their truth when someone else tries to twist it.

Being aware also leads to smarter choices because it allows people to see through manipulation. This kind of independence is important both in our personal lives and at work, where sneaky tactics could otherwise influence our decisions.

This awareness also means we can be more empathetic and supportive of those who have been manipulated. It helps us see the subtle signs of manipulation in others and offers the right help.

When more people understand dark psychology, it creates better, healthier communities and workplaces. It becomes harder for manipulators to get away with their tactics, reducing their impact on groups and organizations.

In short, knowing and understanding dark psychology gives people the power to spot, stand up to, and stop manipulative behavior. This leads to better mental health, smarter decision-making, and stronger, more supportive communities. It's a big step in moving away from the negative effects of manipulation and toward more genuine and healthy interactions.

Moving from understanding the basics, we're now ready to dive into the more detailed aspects of manipulation. This next step takes us from a broad view to a closer look at how manipulation works in real life. The upcoming chapter will dig into the finer points of manipulation, highlight the traits of certain manipulative personalities, and offer clear strategies to deal with and move away from toxic relationships.

CHAPTER 2:

The Art of Manipulation

Imagine you're in a conversation that leaves you feeling uneasy, but you can't pinpoint why. Or perhaps you've agreed to something that, on reflection, doesn't feel entirely right. Have you ever wondered if you've been manipulated? Consider these scenarios:

1. **At Work:** Your boss praises your hard work and suggests you take on an additional project. You agree, feeling flattered, only to realize later that it's not a promotion, but extra work without additional pay.

2. **In a Relationship:** Your partner expresses disappointment every time you spend time with friends, leading you to gradually isolate yourself from your social circle without even realizing it.

3. **In a Family Setting:** A family member often recalls past favors they've done for you, making you feel obligated to meet their current demands.

4. **Online:** You encounter a social media post that evokes a strong emotional response, prompting you to share it without verifying its accuracy.

These examples reflect everyday situations where manipulation could be at play, subtly influencing decisions and emotions. But what exactly is manipulation? Is it always intentional? How does it affect our mental health, and why do people resort to such tactics? This chapter aims to unravel the complex web of manipulation, helping you recognize and navigate these often-invisible influences in your life.

What Is Manipulation?

Manipulation, a complex and often covert strategy, involves influencing or controlling someone's behavior or emotions to benefit the manipulator. This psychological tactic, which ranges from benign persuasion to outright control, is a subtle yet powerful tool in human interactions. At the heart of manipulation lies an imbalance of power, where the manipulator uses deceit or exploitation, often capitalizing on understanding human psychology. They identify motivations, fears, and weaknesses, skillfully using this knowledge to steer decisions or actions to their advantage. Unlike overt coercion, manipulation often goes unnoticed by its targets, leaving them with feelings of unease and confusion but without the awareness of being manipulated. This subtlety makes manipulation both insidious and challenging to recognize and address.

Within the spectrum of awareness in manipulation, some individuals consciously employ manipulative tactics. They understand and calculate their actions, using manipulation as a deliberate strategy for personal gain, control, or self-defense against perceived threats. These individuals plan and execute manipulation with an awareness of its impact, often in a carefully orchestrated manner.

Conversely, manipulation is not always a conscious action. It can manifest as an ingrained behavior, where individuals mimic patterns learned from their environment. In these cases, the manipulator might not fully grasp the manipulative nature of their actions, engaging in these behaviors as a subconscious response to particular situations or triggers.

The process of manipulation typically unfolds through distinct stages, each serving a specific purpose in the manipulative dynamic. Initially, the manipulator works to establish trust or rapport, often through displays of kindness or understanding, to create a connection or dependency. Following this, they gather information about their target's vulnerabilities and motivations, which later becomes a tool for exerting influence. The manipulation intensifies as the exploiter leverages these vulnerabilities, often playing on insecurities or fears, leading the target into a state of obligation or indebtedness.

The ultimate goal of manipulation is control, where the manipulator dictates the target's decisions, emotions, and behaviors, subtly leading them to act against their own interests or desires. To maintain this control, the manipulator continuously exploits vulnerabilities, alternating between positive reinforcement and negative tactics, prolonging their influence and hold over the target.

The motivations driving individuals to engage in manipulative behavior are multifaceted. For some, the primary goal is to get power and control. Others seek personal gain—financial, social, or professional— through manipulative means. Many times, manipulation stems from fear and insecurity; individuals manipulate to secure something they fear losing, whether a relationship, position, or status. Emotional satisfaction, such as the need for attention, validation, or feeling superior, can also drive manipulative behaviors. In certain scenarios, manipulation is a defense mechanism, a tool for individuals who feel threatened, enabling them to protect themselves from harm or confrontation.

Understanding the nuances of manipulation—its definition, the awareness of the manipulator, the progression through various stages, and the underlying motivations—is crucial. It equips us with the knowledge to recognize and counter manipulative tactics in our relationships and interactions, safeguarding our autonomy and well-being.

The Difference Between Persuasion and Manipulation

While both persuasion and manipulation involve influencing others, their core differences lie in their intent, method, and respect for an individual's autonomy.

By promoting open, honest dialogue, we can use persuasion to influence others while respecting their freedom to choose. It involves presenting facts, arguments, and reasoning to help someone make an informed decision. Persuasion is transparent in its intent and seeks a mutually beneficial outcome. For example, a doctor persuading a patient to adopt a healthier lifestyle by presenting the benefits and potential risks is an act of persuasion. It's based on providing information and encouraging the patient to make a decision that aligns with their own values and interests.

In contrast, manipulation often involves deceit, exploitation of vulnerabilities, and a lack of concern for the well-being of the other person. Manipulators have a predetermined outcome in mind and use covert tactics to achieve this outcome. Unlike persuasion, manipulation doesn't necessarily involve an honest or balanced presentation of information. Instead, it often relies on emotional appeals, half-truths, or deceit to influence the other person's decision. For instance, a manipulative salesperson might exaggerate the benefits of a product or withhold information about its downsides, aiming to sway the customer's decision for their gain.

The ethical divide between persuasion and manipulation is significant. Persuasion respects the autonomy and consent of the person being persuaded, whereas manipulation often undermines or violates these principles. Understanding this distinction is crucial in navigating interpersonal communications and recognizing when an attempt to influence crosses the line from respectful persuasion into unethical manipulation.

Decoding Manipulation Techniques

Recognizing the difference between persuasion and manipulation sets the stage for a deeper dive into the various forms of manipulation. Each type of manipulation carries its unique tactics and indicators, and understanding these can be vital in identifying and responding to manipulative behaviors in our daily interactions.

Manipulation comes in many guises and can be encountered in various contexts, from personal relationships to professional environments and even in broader societal interactions. As we delve into these types, we will explore their defining characteristics, how they manifest in real life, and the signs that can help us identify them. This exploration will equip us with the knowledge to not only recognize manipulation when we encounter it but also to understand the mechanisms behind it, allowing us to navigate these situations more effectively and protect ourselves from potential harm.

Types of Manipulation

Manipulation takes many forms, each with its unique characteristics and signs. Recognizing these can be key to understanding and countering manipulative behavior in various contexts.

1. **Lying:** Perhaps the most direct form of manipulation, lying involves presenting false information to deceive others. For example, a colleague might lie about their progress on a project, causing others to make decisions based on incorrect information.

2. **Flattery:** This involves excessive and insincere praise to win favor or influence someone. A classic instance is a salesperson excessively complimenting a client to secure a deal.

3. **Moving the Goalposts:** Here, the manipulator continually changes expectations or rules. In a relationship, this might look like a partner changing their demands just as the other person meets them, keeping them off-balance.

4. **Dodge, Evade, Redirect:** This is about avoiding direct answers or shifting the focus to maintain control or avoid accountability. Politicians often use this tactic during interviews to avoid addressing uncomfortable questions.

5. **Making You the Villain:** This involves shifting blame to the victim, often making them feel responsible for the manipulator's actions. In a workplace setting, a manager might blame an employee for a mistake that was actually the manager's fault.

6. **Isolate and Dominate:** Here, the manipulator cuts off their victim's support systems to gain more control over them. This is common in abusive relationships, where the abuser isolates their partner from friends and family.

7. **Scapegoat:** This tactic involves blaming others for one's own faults or problems. In families, a parent might consistently blame a child for the family's issues.

8. **Control and Coerce Through Lies:** This involves using deception to control someone's actions or decisions. For instance, a friend might lie about a situation to get someone to offer help or support.

9. **Silent Sulk:** Withdrawing communication or affection as control or punishment. For example, a partner may give the "silent treatment" after an argument to exert control.

10. **Negative Reinforcement:** Using criticism or punishment to manipulate someone's behavior. A boss might use constant negative feedback to keep an employee in line.

11. **Blackmail:** This is the use of threats or revealing sensitive information to control someone's actions. An individual might threaten to reveal a friend's secret unless they comply with a demand.

12. **Savior Tactic:** Involves creating a problem to solve and positioning oneself as the hero. A colleague might deliberately cause an issue at work, only to "resolve" it and gain recognition.

Each of these types of manipulation can have profound effects on individuals, leading to stress, reduced self-esteem, and a sense of powerlessness. Recognizing these tactics is the first step toward countering them and protecting oneself from their adverse effects.

Expanding our understanding of manipulation beyond its common forms, we delve into other, perhaps less recognized, but equally impactful types of manipulative behavior. These additional forms often manifest in more specific contexts, requiring a nuanced understanding to identify and address them effectively.

Other Types of Manipulation

Besides the more direct tactics, manipulation can also occur in subtler, more insidious ways. Brainwashing, for instance, is a severe form of manipulation often associated with cults or abusive relationships. It involves the systematic breakdown of an individual's beliefs, perceptions, and identity, replacing them with an alternative set of behaviors or beliefs. This extreme form of manipulation can have lasting psychological impacts, altering a person's sense of self (*Brainwashing Techniques Used by Alienating Parents*, n.d.).

Propaganda represents another sophisticated form of manipulation, commonly used in political or social contexts. It involves spreading biased, misleading, or false information to shape public opinion or behavior. The effectiveness of propaganda lies in its ability to appeal to emotions, biases, or fears, often leading to significant societal impact (Cuncic, 2022a).

In personal relationships, financial manipulation often emerges as a significant form of control, where the manipulator restricts access to funds and exerts influence over the victim's financial decisions (Gillette, 2022). This tactic fosters dependency and complicates the victim's ability to leave the manipulative environment.

In the digital age, cyber manipulation has emerged as a significant concern. Tactics like social engineering attacks involve manipulating individuals into divulging confidential information or performing certain actions, often for fraudulent purposes (*Social Engineering Attack: Hack to Manipulate Psychology*, 2020).

Online trolling and catfishing are other forms of cyber manipulation. Trolling involves posting inflammatory or off-topic messages in online communities to provoke emotional responses (Paglia, 2021). Catfishing, where someone creates a fake identity to deceive others online, often in romantic contexts, can lead to emotional and psychological harm (Wood, 2021).

Each of these forms of manipulation, while distinct, shares a common goal: to influence or control behavior or perceptions, often to the detriment of the victim. Recognizing these various forms of manipulation is crucial in today's world, where such tactics can be found in both personal and digital realms.

Unveiling Manipulation: A Quiz

The ability to identify manipulation is invaluable as we navigate human interactions. The goal of this quiz is to reinforce your understanding of the manipulation forms that we've reviewed. Each question, drawn from real-life scenarios or based on the definitions of manipulative tactics, aims to enhance your awareness and insight into this subtle art.

Read each question carefully and select the most appropriate answer or complete the sentence with the correct term. Remember, manipulation can be subtle and nuanced; hence, each question is an opportunity to sharpen your discernment. Once you've finished the quiz, refer to the answer key at the end of the chapter. It offers detailed explanations and insights for each question, aiding in solidifying your understanding of these complex concepts.

1. During an argument, your partner stops talking to you for days, leaving you feeling guilty and anxious. This behavior is an example of _____.

   a. Silent sulk

   b. Flattery

   c. Savior tactic

   d. Negative reinforcement

2. _____ is a manipulative tactic involving the constant change of rules or expectations to keep someone off-balance.

3. A manager often takes credit for his team's ideas during meetings with senior management. This behavior is an example of

   a. Control and coerce through lies

   b. Moving the goalposts

   c. Making you the villain

d. Scapegoat

4. Using excessive and insincere praise to influence someone's decisions or behavior is known as _____.

5. Every time Mia makes plans with friends, her partner expresses how lonely and sad he feels when she's not around. Mia ends up canceling her plans. This is an example of

    a. Blackmail

    b. Flattery

    c. Emotional blackmail

    d. Negative reinforcement

6. _____ is the tactic of withholding affection or communication to punish or control someone.

7. In a meeting, when asked about a delayed project, a team member diverts the question to discuss a minor success instead. This is a form of

    a. Dodge, evade, redirect

    b. Lying

    c. Savior tactic

    d. Negative reinforcement

8. After a disagreement, your colleague implies that if you don't support their idea, you might not be considered a "team player." This is an example of

    a. Control and coerce through lies

    b. Moving the goalposts

    c. Making you the villain

    d. Scapegoat

As we transition from understanding the how of manipulation, our next chapter will introduce us to the who—the personalities most prone to employing these manipulative tactics. This next chapter promises to deepen our understanding of the human elements behind manipulation, offering insights into the psychological profiles that often underpin such behaviors.

Answer Key

1. **Silent Sulk:** This manipulation tactic involves withdrawing communication, often as a means of control or punishment. By refusing to speak or engage, the manipulator exerts power by creating a sense of uncertainty and unease. This tactic can be particularly damaging as it forces the victim into a position of vulnerability in order to seek reconciliation or clarity.

2. **Moving the Goalposts:** A common method where manipulators continually change their expectations or requirements. This tactic leaves the victim in a perpetual state of trying to meet shifting standards, often feeling inadequate or unsuccessful. Understanding this tactic helps you recognize the futility of trying to satisfy these ever-changing demands.

3. **Control and Coerce Through Lies:** Taking credit for others' work is a deceitful means of control. It involves not only a blatant lie but also a manipulation of the perception of others. Recognizing this tactic can empower you to challenge such unjust claims and protect your work and contributions.

4. **Flattery:** Often used in manipulation, this tactic involves giving insincere praise to influence someone's behavior or decisions. While it may seem harmless, flattery can be a subtle way to disarm and manipulate, leading individuals to lower their guard and become more susceptible to influence.

5. **Emotional Blackmail:** This manipulation tactic involves playing on someone's emotions of guilt, fear, or sympathy to control their actions. It's a form of psychological manipulation that preys on the victim's emotional weaknesses and insecurities.

6. **Dodge, Evade, Redirect:** This involves avoiding direct answers or responsibilities to maintain control or evade accountability. By doing so, the manipulator keeps the other person confused and off-balance, unable to get a straight answer or resolution.

7. **Manipulative Misdirection:** A tactic where a manipulator diverts attention from a critical issue to a less relevant or positive topic, preventing resolution and maintaining control.

8. **Making You the Villain:** In this form of manipulation, the manipulator makes someone feel guilty or wrong for opposing their views or actions. It's a way of deflecting attention and responsibility away from themselves by making the other person question their own behavior and intentions.

By understanding these manipulation tactics, you are better equipped to identify and respond to them effectively. Recognizing these patterns is the first step in asserting your autonomy and protecting yourself from manipulative influences. Remember, knowledge is power, and, in this case, it's your shield against those who seek to use dark psychology against you.

CHAPTER 3:

Meet the Personalities

Imagine a world where charm masks deceit, ambition conceals exploitation, and charisma hides emotional coldness. That world is where the dark triad of personality traits resides—a realm where narcissism, Machiavellianism, and psychopathy interweave to create complex human behaviors that challenge our understanding of ethics, empathy, and interpersonal relationships.

Recent studies have peeled back layers of these traits, revealing a rich tapestry far more intricate than previously thought. These traits, while distinct, often overlap, creating unique behavioral patterns that impact personal and professional environments (Heym & Sumich, 2022).

In this chapter, we set off on a quest to decode these puzzling characters. We will explore not just their surface traits, but try to understand the depths of their interactions, influences, and the subtle nuances that differentiate them. By understanding these personalities, we gain insights into a range of behaviors, from the seemingly innocuous to the overtly harmful, enhancing our ability to navigate complex social landscapes.

What Is the Dark Tetrad?

As we continue into the depths of personality psychology, we come across the dark tetrad, which expands upon the well-known dark triad. To start, let's examine these fascinating psychological concepts that help make sense of perplexing and occasionally disruptive human behavior.

The Dark Triad: Its Origins and Expansion to Tetrad

The dark triad, which we said includes narcissism, Machiavellianism, and psychopathy, has fascinated psychologists and the public because of its important implications in different areas of life. Each of these traits, though distinct, shares common threads of self-centeredness, manipulation, and a lack of empathy.

The expansion to the dark tetrad came with including sadism, a trait characterized by deriving pleasure from inflicting pain, suffering, or humiliation on others. The addition of sadism to the triad acknowledges that the enjoyment of cruelty can be an integral part of these destructive personality constellations.

Commonality and Identification

Contrary to the notion that these traits are rare or only present in extreme cases, research suggests that elements of the dark triad are more common in the general population than previously thought (Dolan, 2021). While not everyone exhibits these traits to a pathological degree, many individuals may display them in more subdued forms, affecting their relationships and social interactions.

Identifying these traits in individuals can be challenging, as people often mask their manipulative and harmful tendencies. Narcissists, for example, might hide their vulnerability and insecurity behind a facade of confidence and charm. Machiavellians might appear cooperative and trustworthy, only to reveal their true intentions when it serves their purpose. Psychopaths can be charming and persuasive, making it difficult to see their lack of empathy and remorse. Sadists may blend in socially, with their enjoyment of others' pain not immediately apparent.

Relationships With Dark Triad Personalities

Building relationships with people who display these characteristics can be particularly challenging. The manipulative and self-serving nature of these personalities means that they often leave a wake of strained relationships and emotional turmoil. Consider the case of Emma, who found herself constantly undermined and criticized by her partner, a typical narcissist. His need for admiration and affirmation, coupled with a lack of empathy, left her feeling emotionally drained and undervalued.

In professional settings, these traits can manifest in ways that disrupt teamwork and ethical conduct. A Machiavellian leader, for instance, might manipulate team members to pit them against each other in order to ensure their own power and control within the organization.

Understanding these traits and their impact is crucial, not just for mental health professionals but for anyone navigating complex social landscapes. Recognizing the signs and learning to interact with individuals exhibiting these traits can help mitigate their negative impact on personal and professional relationships.

Now, it's time to explore the different personalities within the tetrad.

Narcissism: Unveiling the Facade of Grandiosity

Narcissism, a term often associated with self-absorption and a grandiose sense of self-importance, represents a complex personality trait with far-reaching implications. At its core, narcissism revolves around an inflated sense of self-worth, a deep need for admiration, and a notable lack of empathy for others.

Understanding Narcissism

The concept of narcissism originates from the Greek myth of Narcissus, a young man who fell in love with his reflection. In psychological terms, narcissism is more than just self-love or vanity; it's a pattern of thinking and behavior characterized by a pervasive sense of grandiosity, a chronic need for admiration, and a lack of empathy.

People with narcissistic traits often present a facade of confidence and superiority. However, this outward appearance usually masks a fragile self-esteem that is vulnerable to the slightest criticism. They may seek constant validation and attention from others to support their self-image.

Signs of Narcissism

Recognizing narcissism can be challenging, especially as narcissists are often charismatic, especially in initial encounters. Key signs include

- a grandiose sense of self-importance
- preoccupations with fantasies of unlimited success, power, brilliance, beauty, or ideal love
- a belief that they are "special"
- a need for excessive admiration
- a sense of entitlement and expectation of favorable treatment
- exploitative behavior in relationships
- a lack of empathy
- envy toward others or a belief that others are envious of them
- arrogant and haughty behaviors or attitudes

Consider the case of Michael, a high-level executive known for his charisma and confidence. On the surface, he appeared successful and was admired by his peers. However, this facade concealed a deep-seated narcissism. Michael constantly sought validation and admiration from his colleagues and was quick to take credit for successes while blaming others for failures. His inability to empathize with his team members led to a toxic work environment, characterized by high turnover and low morale.

Causes and Emotional Impact

The causes of narcissism are thought to be multifactorial, involving a complex interplay of genetic, psychological, and environmental factors. Childhood experiences, such as excessive pampering or, conversely, excessive criticism, may contribute to the development of narcissistic traits.

The emotional impact of interacting with a narcissist can be profound. Relationships with narcissists are often one-sided and emotionally draining. They can leave individuals feeling undervalued, misunderstood, and disregarded. Narcissists' lack of empathy and tendency to exploit others can result in significant emotional pain and psychological distress for those close to them.

Understanding narcissism is crucial for those who find themselves in relationships, whether personal or professional, with individuals exhibiting these traits. It can provide insights into the dynamics of these relationships and strategies for managing interactions more effectively.

The Art of Cunning and Deception: Machiavellianism Unveiled

Machiavellianism, named after the Renaissance diplomat Niccolò Machiavelli, represents a personality characterized by a cold pragmatism, a strategic manipulation of others, and often a blatant disregard for morality. Individuals with high Machiavellian traits are skilled in the art of deceit and often use cunning tactics to achieve their ends, making this personality type challenging in interpersonal relationships and societal interactions.

The Nature of Machiavellianism

At its heart, Machiavellianism is about manipulation and the strategic use of others for personal gain. It involves a cynical view of human nature and a belief that ends often justify the means, regardless of the ethical implications. This trait is associated with a focus on self-interest, deception, and the exploitation of others.

Identifying Machiavellian Traits

Recognizing Machiavellianism can be challenging, as individuals with these traits are often adept at blending in and masking their intentions. Key characteristics include

- a tendency to deceive and manipulate others for personal gain

- a cynical disregard for morality and a focus on self-interest

- a capacity for extended emotional detachment and a calculated approach to relationships

- a strategic and often ruthless focus on achieving objectives

- a lack of empathy and an inclination to exploit others

Meet Marcus, a team leader in a tech company who is renowned for his innovative approaches and results-driven mindset. On the surface, Marcus was admired for his quick decision-making and seemingly effective team management. However, beneath this veneer of success lay a more unsettling reality. Marcus had a knack for subtly undermining his team members, often setting them up in competitive scenarios that bred distrust and rivalry, all under the guise of fostering a dynamic work environment. His strategy involved discreetly shifting responsibilities and credit, ensuring he remained indispensable and in control. This approach, while initially unnoticed, gradually eroded team morale and led to a significant decline in collaborative spirit and productivity.

Causes and Impact on Relationships

The development of Machiavellian traits is believed to be shaped by both genetics and the environment. Exposure to certain family dynamics, societal influences, or specific life experiences can contribute to the development of these traits.

The impact of Machiavellianism on relationships is often negative, marked by trust issues and emotional distress. Interactions with a Machiavellian individual can leave one feeling used and manipulated, with a sense of betrayal and mistrust. In professional settings, this can lead to a toxic work environment characterized by a lack of genuine teamwork and an atmosphere of suspicion and competition.

Understanding these traits can be key to navigating relationships and environments where these characteristics are present. Recognizing the signs can help in developing strategies to protect oneself from manipulation and foster healthier interaction patterns.

Psychopathy: Understanding the Nature of a Misunderstood Trait

The complex personality trait of psychopathy is often misunderstood and sensationalized. It involves a lack of empathy, shallow emotions, and a preference for manipulative and occasionally antisocial behavior.

Defining Psychopathy

Psychopathy is more than the dramatic portrayal often seen in media; it's a nuanced personality disorder marked by specific behavioral and emotional characteristics. Key features of psychopathy include

- a lack of remorse or guilt

- emotional shallowness and a lack of empathy

- superficial charm and glibness

- impulsivity and irresponsibility

- a propensity for deceit and manipulation

- a tendency toward antisocial and risky behaviors

Unlike the popular depiction of psychopaths as inherently violent or criminal, many individuals with psychopathic traits can function in society, often undetected. They may use their charm and manipulative skills to achieve success in various fields, sometimes at the expense of others.

An illustrative example is John, a seemingly charismatic and successful businessman. His charm and confidence made him well-liked in social circles. However, beneath this veneer, John exhibited classic traits of psychopathy: He manipulated business partners without remorse, lied effortlessly, and showed a complete disregard for the consequences of his actions on others. His relationships were superficial, serving only his interests and gains.

Causes and Behavioral Impact

The causes of psychopathy are complex and not fully understood. Research suggests a combination of genetic predispositions and environmental factors, such as childhood experiences and family dynamics, contribute to the development of psychopathic traits.

The impact of psychopathy on relationships is profound. Interactions with a psychopath can be confusing and harmful, as their lack of empathy and manipulative tendencies often lead to emotional harm and betrayal. In professional settings, a psychopath's manipulative and risky behaviors can create a disruptive and potentially harmful work environment.

Relationships With Psychopaths

Dealing with individuals who exhibit psychopathic traits requires awareness and caution. Understanding these traits can help in recognizing potentially manipulative and harmful behaviors and in developing strategies to protect oneself. It's important to set boundaries, avoid emotional entanglement, and seek support when dealing with individuals showing signs of psychopathy.

The Dark Side of Pleasure in Pain: Unraveling Sadism

The fourth and often overlooked component of the dark tetrad is a disturbing yet critical personality trait to understanding dark psychology. Unlike the other elements of the tetrad, which are characterized by emotional detachment, sadism is distinctly defined as deriving pleasure from the suffering of others.

Sadism goes beyond mere cruelty; it is characterized by finding pleasure or satisfaction in inflicting pain, suffering, or humiliation on others. While it can manifest in physical forms, sadism can also be psychological, involving emotional manipulation and degradation.

Identifying Sadistic Traits

Recognizing sadistic tendencies can be challenging, as these behaviors are often concealed or rationalized. Key characteristics include

- enjoyment or pleasure in causing physical or psychological pain to others

- fascination with witnessing others' suffering

- manipulation or control of others leading to painful or humiliating situations

- a lack of empathy and remorse in relation to the suffering inflicted

An example of sadism in a professional context could be a supervisor who takes pleasure in demeaning or humiliating employees. Consider the case of Linda, a manager known for her harsh and critical management style. She would often belittle her team members publicly, finding satisfaction in their discomfort and distress. This behavior not only created a toxic workplace environment but also led to significant emotional distress among her employees.

Causes and Emotional Impact

The development of sadistic traits is not fully understood, but it is thought to involve a complex interplay of psychological, environmental, and possibly genetic factors. Exposure to violence or abusive behavior in early life, for example, may contribute to the development of sadistic tendencies.

The emotional impact of interacting with a sadistic individual can be profound and damaging. Victims may experience fear, anxiety, and a sense of helplessness, leading to long-term psychological harm. In relationships, whether personal or professional, sadistic behavior can lead to a climate of fear and mistrust.

Navigating Relationships With Sadistic Personalities

Engaging with individuals who exhibit sadistic traits requires awareness and a cautious approach. Understanding these traits can help in recognizing the signs of sadistic behavior and in taking steps to protect oneself from potential harm. Setting clear boundaries, seeking support from others, and avoiding situations that empower the sadistic individual are crucial strategies for those who find themselves in relationships with such personalities.

Related Disorders: The Intricate Web of Conditions Associated With the Dark Tetrad

In the complex landscape of personality psychology, the dark tetrad traits do not exist in isolation. They often intersect with various related disorders, each adding layers to our understanding of these challenging personality profiles. We want to review conditions closely associated with the dark tetrad, illuminating their similarities, differences, and the intricate ways they manifest in behavior.

Antisocial Personality Disorder

Antisocial personality disorder (ASPD) shares several characteristics with psychopathy, a core component of the dark tetrad. Marked by a long-term pattern of disregard for other people's rights, individuals with ASPD often demonstrate behaviors that are deceitful, manipulative, and devoid of remorse. Unlike the broader spectrum of psychopathy, ASPD is specifically defined and diagnosed based on behavioral patterns and interactions with others and the law.

Consider the case of Jack, known in his community for his charm and wit. However, his close acquaintances have witnessed a different side: a propensity for lying, a tendency to violate others' rights without guilt, and repeated run-ins with the law. Jack's behavior aligns with ASPD, illustrating the disorder's complex interplay with dark triad traits, particularly psychopathy.

The MacDonald Triad: A Window Into Early Behavioral Concerns

The MacDonald Triad, theorized to be an indicator of future violent behavior, includes three behaviors: cruelty to animals, obsession with fire setting, and persistent bedwetting. While not a conclusive predictor of future psychopathy or sociopathy, the triad suggests potential developmental concerns that could develop into more serious antisocial behavior. Early interventions in children exhibiting these behaviors may help in mitigating the risk of developing more severe antisocial traits.

Conduct Disorder: The Precursor to ASPD

We can see conduct disorder in children and adolescents as a precursor to ASPD. Characterized by a repetitive and persistent pattern of behavior violating the basic rights of others or major age-appropriate societal norms, this disorder includes aggression toward people and animals, destruction of property, deceitfulness, theft, and serious violations of rules.

Think of a teenager like Liam, known at school for his aggressive behavior, frequent fights, and blatant disrespect for authority. Such patterns of behavior in adolescence might grow into ASPD if not addressed.

Subclinical Traits

Subclinical traits refer to the presence of dark tetrad characteristics that do not meet the full criteria for a clinical diagnosis. These traits manifest in less intense forms but can still significantly impact interpersonal relationships and personal well-being. For instance, an individual might exhibit narcissistic tendencies, like seeking excessive admiration and exhibiting a sense of entitlement, without the full spectrum of narcissistic personality disorder (NPD).

Dealing with someone who has subclinical dark tetrad traits can be subtly challenging. Their behavior may not be overtly destructive but can still cause emotional and psychological strain in relationships, often leaving others feeling confused, undervalued, or manipulated.

Understanding these related disorders is crucial in comprehending the full spectrum of the dark tetrad traits. Each disorder adds a layer of complexity to the psychological profile of individuals exhibiting these traits, making it essential to approach them with a nuanced understanding. This knowledge not only helps in identifying these traits and disorders, but also in developing effective strategies for interaction and, where possible, intervention.

Can It Be Cured?

As we navigate the intricate pathways of the dark tetrad and its related disorders, a pressing question emerges: Can these deeply ingrained personality traits and behaviors be "cured" or significantly mitigated? This exploration delves into the possibilities and limitations of therapeutic interventions for individuals exhibiting these complex traits.

Addressing the dark tetrad traits—narcissism, Machiavellianism, psychopathy, and sadism—along with related disorders like ASPD, poses a significant challenge. These traits are often deeply rooted in an individual's personality and are not typically considered "illnesses" that can be cured in the traditional sense. However, there are interventions that can help manage these traits and reduce their impact on both the individuals who possess them and those around them.

Therapeutic Interventions: Strategies and Limitations

Therapeutic approaches to addressing these traits often involve a combination of psychotherapy, behavior modification techniques, and, sometimes, medication to manage specific symptoms or concurrent mental health issues. Cognitive-behavioral therapy (CBT) and dialectical behavior therapy (DBT) are commonly used to help individuals recognize and modify harmful thought patterns and behaviors.

However, the success of these interventions largely depends on the individual's willingness and ability to engage with the therapeutic process. For example, individuals with strong narcissistic traits might find it challenging to acknowledge their vulnerabilities or engage in therapy, as this could be perceived as a threat to their self-image (Brenner, 2021).

With ASPD, treatment is challenging because of the inherent lack of empathy and remorse. However, early intervention, especially in adolescents showing signs of conduct disorder, can be crucial in preventing the development of more severe antisocial behaviors.

Subclinical Traits: A Window for Intervention

For those with subclinical traits, the prospects of intervention are more promising. Since these traits are less severe and rigid, individuals might be more amenable to therapy and behavioral interventions. Early recognition and intervention can play a significant role in mitigating the development and impact of these traits.

The Role of Professional Therapy

Professional therapy is crucial to address these complex personality traits and related disorders. It's important to emphasize that individuals should not attempt to "cure" these traits in themselves or others without professional guidance. Psychotherapy can provide the tools and support needed to understand and manage these traits but should be conducted by qualified mental health professionals.

The process of therapy can be long and requires commitment and patience, both from the therapist and the individual. Success here is not solely dependent on a complete personality transformation, but also on improvements in behavior management, relationship quality, and overall functioning.

Unraveling the Dark Tapestry

We've traversed the intricate and often shadowy paths of complex personality traits. Our exploration has brought to light the multifaceted nature of human behaviors that veer into the darker aspects of psychology. We've gained a deeper understanding of how these traits not only shape individual characters but also affect the fabric of relationships and social dynamics.

This journey into understanding has been more than an academic foray; it has provided practical insights into navigating the challenging waters of interactions with those who exhibit these traits. From the nuances of manipulation to the subtleties of strategic self-interest, our exploration has shed light on the often-hidden mechanisms of human behavior.

Now, we turn our focus to a specific aspect of this complex tapestry. The next part of our exploration delves deeper into one particular trait that stands out for its prevalence and impact. Here, we'll unravel the layers of a personality trait characterized by its paradox of fragility and grandiosity, seeking to understand its influence on both personal development and interpersonal relationships.

CHAPTER 4:

The Mind of a Narcissist

In the heart of Greek mythology lies the tale of Narcissus, a story that has transcended time, offering a poignant metaphor for self-absorption and vanity.

Narcissus, known for his extraordinary beauty, encounters his reflection in a pool of water and becomes utterly enamored with it. So intense is his infatuation that he cannot draw himself away, ultimately leading to his tragic downfall. This story, rooted in mythology, strikingly encapsulates the core elements of narcissism: a profound absorption with oneself and a lack of connection to the external world.

This mythological narrative serves as a metaphor for understanding NPD in contemporary psychology. Narcissus's inability to look beyond his reflection mirrors the emotional and psychological landscape of individuals with NPD—a condition marked by an inflated sense of self-importance, a deep need for excessive attention and admiration, and a lack of empathy for others.

The relevance of Narcissus's story to modern-day interpretations of narcissism is significant. It symbolizes the self-destructive nature of extreme self-centeredness, a theme that resonates in the psychological profiles of those grappling with NPD. As we delve deeper into the dynamics of narcissistic behavior, the image of Narcissus gazing into the water serves as a constant reminder of the psychological complexities we aim to unravel.

This ancient tale sets the foundation for our journey into understanding narcissism, from its mythological representations to its clinical manifestations. As we move forward, we will explore the prevalence, origins, and characteristics of NPD, piecing together how this ancient myth reflects modern psychological realities.

A Closer Look Into Narcissism

Narcissism, once perceived as a rare and extreme personality flaw, has emerged as a more commonly recognized trait in contemporary society. This shift in perception aligns with research showing a broader spectrum of narcissistic behavior prevalent among the general population. A study suggests that while extreme cases, categorized as NPD, remain relatively uncommon, subclinical forms of narcissism are more widespread (Peisley, 2017). This prevalence is significant, suggesting that narcissistic traits, ranging from benign self-focus to severe self-absorption and entitlement, are more common than previously understood.

The rise of digital culture and social media has amplified visibility and perhaps even the normalization of narcissistic tendencies. Platforms that encourage self-promotion and validation-seeking behaviors provide fertile ground for the expression and reinforcement of narcissistic traits. This societal shift prompts us to reevaluate how we view narcissism—not just as a clinical disorder, but as a spectrum of behaviors influenced by cultural and social factors.

Historical Context and Freud's Contributions

The journey to understand and categorize narcissism as a psychological disorder has deep historical roots. Sigmund Freud was among the first to explore narcissism through the lens of psychoanalysis. He posited that narcissism was a natural phase in human development but also recognized that some individuals remained fixated at this stage, leading to pathological narcissism (Cherry, 2019). Freud's theories laid the groundwork for future psychologists to delve deeper into the nuances of narcissistic behaviors and their impact on individual and interpersonal dynamics.

Freud's view of narcissism as a developmental phase was pivotal, as it suggested both the universality and potential pathology of narcissistic traits. This dual perspective fostered a deeper exploration into how narcissism could manifest healthily and problematically within individuals.

The formal recognition of narcissism as a distinct psychological disorder occurred in the latter half of the 20th century. This period marked a shift from understanding narcissism solely as a personality trait to categorizing it as a diagnosable condition—NPD. Including NPD in diagnostic manuals like the Diagnostic and Statistical Manual of Mental Disorders (DSM) was a critical step in differentiating it from other personality disorders and acknowledging its unique set of symptoms and behaviors.

The recognition of NPD facilitated more focused research and understanding of the disorder. It established a basis for mental health professionals to identify and address individuals displaying pathological narcissistic tendencies, marked by persistent patterns of exaggerated self-importance, an intense desire for admiration, and an absence of empathy.

With this historical exploration, I aim to reveal the dynamic evolution of the concept from a developmental phase and personality trait to a recognized psychological disorder. Understanding this evolution is essential for comprehensively grasping the complexities of narcissistic behaviors and their implications in modern society.

Understanding NPD

Understanding NPD requires delving into its specific characteristics, how it differs in men and women, and its various subtypes. Here, I want to paint a clearer picture of how NPD manifests and affects individuals and those around them.

Defining NPD

Several key characteristics define NPD. Individuals with this disorder often display an exaggerated sense of their own importance, underpinned by an unstable sense of self-worth. They require excessive admiration and validation and may become preoccupied with fantasies of success, power, or beauty. Crucially, they often display a lack of empathy, struggling to recognize or identify with the feelings and needs of others.

These traits manifest in behaviors that are arrogant or haughty and relationships that are largely superficial and exploitative. The self-esteem of a narcissist is usually delicate. This vulnerability can lead to defensive reactions, such as anger or disdain, when their self-image is threatened (Kim, 2023).

Differences for Men and Women With NPD

NPD tends to manifest distinctly in men compared to women. Men with NPD often display more blatant forms of excessive self-regard and a strong sense of entitlement. They may be more aggressive in their pursuit of admiration and more openly display their perceived superiority. In contrast, women with NPD might display these traits in more subtle and covert ways. Their narcissism may be expressed through a heightened sensitivity to how others perceive them and a more manipulative form of self-promotion and attention-seeking.

These gender differences in NPD are crucial for understanding how the disorder is experienced and perceived by the individual and those around them. They also have implications for diagnosis and treatment, as the more subtle manifestations of NPD in women may be less easily recognized or may be misinterpreted.

Narcissism Subordinate Types

NPD encompasses several subordinate types, each presenting unique characteristics:

1. **The Grandiose Narcissist:** This is the most commonly recognized form, characterized by overt expressions of superiority and entitlement. Individuals in this category are often extroverted, assertive, and attention-seeking.

2. **The Vulnerable Narcissist:** Also known as covert narcissism, this subtype is less obvious. Individuals with this form of NPD may appear shy, sensitive, or withdrawn. They harbor grandiose fantasies but are more inhibited in their behavior and more sensitive to how others view them.

3. **The Malignant Narcissist:** Traits that overlap with ASPD, including manipulativeness, a lack of empathy, and sadistic behaviors characterize this subtype. Malignant narcissists are often aggressive, ruthless, and unapologetically exploitative.

Each subtype presents its own set of challenges in interpersonal relationships and requires specific approaches in therapy and interaction.

Diagnosing and Treating NPD

Diagnosing NPD involves a thorough evaluation by a mental health professional. This process typically includes a detailed clinical interview, psychological testing, and a review of the individual's history. The criteria outlined in the DSM serve as a guideline. Clinicians look for persistent patterns of grandiosity, need for admiration, and lack of empathy that significantly impair an individual's ability to function in personal and professional settings.

However, diagnosing NPD can be complex because of several factors. Individuals with NPD often lack insight into their condition and may not see their traits as problematic. They may also be reluctant to seek help or be defensive and resistant during the evaluation process. These challenges need a nuanced approach to diagnosis, often requiring multiple sessions and a comprehensive evaluation of the individual's behavior across different contexts.

What Causes NPD?

NPD is believed to result from the intricate interplay of genetic, environmental, and psychological factors. While there isn't a single cause, several contributing elements have been identified:

- **Genetic Factors:** Research suggests a potential genetic component to NPD, although specific genes have not been conclusively identified.

- **Early Childhood Experiences:** Experiences in childhood, such as excessive pampering, unrealistic expectations from parents, or emotional abuse, can contribute to the development of narcissistic traits.

- **Personality Development:** The formation of personality and self-identity during developmental stages plays a significant role in the emergence of NPD.

Understanding these causes is essential for developing effective treatment strategies and for providing support to individuals with NPD and their families.

Treatment Strategies for NPD

Treatment for NPD is challenging and often requires a long-term commitment. The primary mode of treatment is psychotherapy, with the goal of helping individuals understand their emotions, develop healthier self-esteem, and improve their relationships. However, individuals with NPD may have difficulty recognizing the need for change or may be resistant to the therapeutic process. Key components of treatment often include

- **CBT:** CBT is used to address the distorted thinking patterns and beliefs that underlie narcissistic behaviors. It helps individuals develop more realistic self-perceptions and healthier ways of interacting with others.

- **Psychodynamic Therapy:** This approach explores the underlying unconscious motivations and early childhood experiences that contribute to narcissistic behaviors, aiming to foster insight and change.

- **Group Therapy:** In some cases, group therapy can be beneficial, providing a space for individuals with NPD to learn from others and practice empathy and interpersonal skills.

While medication is not typically used to treat NPD directly, it may be prescribed to address co-occurring issues, such as depression or anxiety.

However, the treatment of NPD is often a complex and lengthy process. The ingrained nature of narcissistic traits means that significant and lasting change can take time. Treatment success is measured not just by the reduction of narcissistic behaviors, but also by improvements in the individual's relationships and overall functioning.

One of the critical challenges in treating NPD is the individual's resistance to acknowledging their vulnerabilities and engaging in the therapeutic process. Building a therapeutic alliance where the individual feels understood and supported is crucial for effective treatment. Therapists often need to balance empathy with setting boundaries and challenging the individual's maladaptive behaviors.

Why Can Narcissistic Behavior Be Harmful?

The exploration of narcissistic behavior reveals that it has implications that reach beyond mere self-absorption or a craving for attention. The essence of narcissism, as we've explored, lies in a deeply rooted psychological pattern that significantly impacts interpersonal relationships and societal structures. This examination focuses on the reasons behind narcissistic actions, the cognitive workings of narcissists, and the tangible effects of their behavior in real-life scenarios.

The Complex Psychology Behind Narcissistic Actions

Narcissism manifests in behaviors that significantly impact interpersonal relationships and societal dynamics.

As we've explored, narcissism is fundamentally defined by an exaggerated self-importance, often concealing underlying insecurity and vulnerability. This dichotomy drives the narcissist's constant need for admiration and validation. Narcissists create and maintain a facade of superiority, which is crucial for their self-esteem but often leads to problematic interactions with others. In a workplace setting, a narcissistic manager may demand unwavering loyalty and praise from their team, creating an environment where dissent is not tolerated and the manager's need for recognition overshadows individual contributions. This situation has the potential to dampen creativity and morale, making employees feel undervalued and demotivated.

The lack of empathy is a defining characteristic of narcissistic behavior. This deficiency in understanding and valuing others' feelings results in relationships that are skewed, with the narcissist's needs and desires taking precedence. In personal relationships, this dynamic can be particularly damaging. Partners of narcissists often find themselves in a perpetual cycle of trying to appease the narcissist, only to be met with indifference or disdain. Over time, these partners may experience a decline in their self-esteem and sense of self-worth, as their own needs and emotions are continually dismissed or invalidated.

Narcissistic thought patterns contribute significantly to their harmful behavior. Narcissists often engage in grandiose fantasies about their own success and superiority. These are not mere daydreams; they are essential for maintaining their fragile self-esteem. Narcissists also tend to think in extremes, categorizing people and situations as entirely good or bad, superior or inferior. Binary thinking disregards relationship nuances, causing demeaning behavior.

Defensive mechanisms are another critical aspect of the narcissistic mindset. In an effort to protect their delicate sense of self-worth, narcissists might refute their shortcomings, attribute their insecurities to others, and justify their actions. This defense strategy often manifests as blame-shifting, where the narcissist attributes their shortcomings and mistakes to external factors or other people, avoiding any responsibility or introspection.

The impact of narcissistic behavior extends beyond personal relationships to wider societal implications. In leadership roles, narcissistic individuals may prioritize personal ambitions over ethical considerations and collective well-being. Their focus on self-promotion and personal gain can result in decisions and actions detrimental to groups, organizations, or entire communities.

The psychology behind narcissistic actions reveals a pattern of behavior driven by an unstable self-image, a lack of empathy, and defensive thought processes. These characteristics lead to a range of harmful outcomes, affecting not only those in close relationships with narcissists but also broader societal structures. Recognizing and understanding these dynamics is crucial for navigating interactions with narcissists and mitigating their impact.

Narcissistic Thought Patterns: A Cognitive Insight

Exploring the cognitive landscape of narcissistic individuals unveils a complex network of thought patterns that underpin their behavior. These mental processes are not just superficial traits but deeply ingrained ways of thinking that significantly influence how narcissists perceive themselves and interact with the world.

Central to the narcissist's cognitive framework is a grandiose sense of self. This is often manifested in exaggerated perceptions of their abilities and achievements, and a constant need for admiration and affirmation. However, this apparent grandeur often conceals an underlying self-esteem that is acutely vulnerable to criticism or perceived affronts. This vulnerability is often concealed behind a veneer of confidence and superiority, creating a cycle of needing constant validation to maintain their self-image.

The way narcissists process information and experiences often involves a significant degree of distortion. They may interpret benign actions or comments as personal attacks or see themselves as the victim in situations where they are not. This distortion extends to how they view others, often underestimating or devaluing people whom they perceive as threats to their self-esteem.

Narcissists also engage in black-and-white thinking, categorizing people and situations into extremes. They may oscillate between seeing themselves as flawless and feeling utterly worthless, with little room for a realistic self-assessment. This binary thinking extends to their relationships, where they may idealize individuals who admire them and devalue those who critique them.

Another critical aspect of the narcissistic thought pattern is the propensity for fantasy. Narcissists often indulge in fantasies about unlimited success, power, or beauty to compensate for the gaps between their ideals and reality. These fantasies can be a source of motivation but can also detach them from the practicalities and responsibilities of real life.

Defensive mechanisms play a crucial role in the narcissist's cognitive functioning. To protect their fragile ego, narcissists often resort to denial, projection, and rationalization. They might deny any flaws or mistakes and project their negative traits onto others, accusing them of the very faults they refuse to acknowledge in themselves. Rationalization allows them to justify their behavior, often in ways that align with their inflated self-perception.

These cognitive patterns contribute significantly to the harmful nature of narcissistic behavior. The lack of empathy, the need for admiration, and the inability to deal with criticism or failure can lead to behaviors that are damaging both to the narcissists themselves and those around them. Understanding these thought patterns is essential for comprehending the challenges of interacting with narcissistic individuals and for professionals who work toward treating them.

The Ripple Effect of Narcissistic Behavior in Society

The impact of narcissistic behavior is most immediately felt in personal relationships. Individuals with narcissistic tendencies can create unbalanced dynamics, marked by a lack of genuine reciprocity and empathy. Partners, family members, or close associates often find themselves in positions where their needs and feelings are secondary to the narcissist's. This can lead to strained relationships, where manipulation and emotional volatility are prevalent. For example, a narcissistic parent might impose unreasonable expectations on their children, valuing their achievements only as extensions of their own self-worth, leading to long-term emotional repercussions for the children.

In professional settings, narcissistic behavior can significantly disrupt the normal flow of operations and relationships. A narcissistic leader or colleague might prioritize personal agendas and recognition over collaborative success and the well-being of the team. Such behavior can manifest as exploiting subordinates, taking credit for others' work, or undermining colleagues to maintain a sense of superiority. The result is often a toxic work environment characterized by high stress, low morale, and a culture that stifles innovation and healthy communication.

On a broader societal level, narcissism can influence cultural norms and values. In leadership roles, be it in corporate, political, or social spheres, individuals with strong narcissistic traits can shape policies and decisions that reflect their personal interests rather than the collective good. Their leadership approach may be defined by authoritarianism, lack of transparency, and unethical practices, all of which can profoundly affect communities and societies.

Additionally, in a culture influenced by social media and celebrities, narcissistic behavior can become glamorous or accepted. This could lead to a societal change where empathy, humility, and cooperation lose value, and self-promotion and competition are praised. Such a shift can alter the fabric of social interactions and communal living, prioritizing individual success over communal well-being.

Recognizing the ripple effect of narcissistic behavior is the first step in mitigating its impact. For individuals in personal or professional relationships with narcissists, this means setting boundaries, seeking support, and prioritizing one's emotional well-being. For organizations, this entails cultivating environments that emphasize empathy and teamwork rather than personal self-promotion. On a societal level, it calls for a collective awareness of the detrimental effects of glorifying narcissistic traits and an active effort to promote healthier, more inclusive values.

From Understanding to Recognition

We have navigated the landscape of NPD understanding its deep-seated roots and the multifaceted ways it manifests and impacts both individuals and society. This exploration has uncovered the intricate psychological fabric of narcissism from the grandiose self-perceptions and fragile egos to the lack of empathy that characterizes this condition. We've seen how these traits unfold in personal and professional relationships, creating challenging dynamics and often leading to strained, unbalanced interactions.

By examining the cognitive realm of narcissism, we've explored the thought processes behind narcissistic behaviors. We have examined the tendency of individuals with NPD to oscillate between extreme self-adulation and vulnerability, their black-and-white view of the world, and their defensive mechanisms to protect their fragile self-esteem. These cognitive traits not only define the behavior of narcissists but also explain why their actions can be so impactful and damaging.

Beyond personal relationships, the ripple effects of narcissistic behavior in wider social and professional contexts have been one of our focal points. Narcissism's impact on workplace dynamics, leadership styles, and broader societal norms and values has been highlighted, underscoring the importance of awareness and understanding of these behaviors in various settings.

As we transition from understanding the intricacies of NPD to recognizing its outward signs, the next chapter promises to be an essential guide. It aims to equip you with the knowledge to identify narcissistic behaviors in different contexts. This understanding is crucial, not just for personal empowerment and protection but also for fostering healthier interactions and relationships in both personal and professional spheres.

The upcoming chapter will build on the foundation laid here, moving from the theoretical and psychological aspects of narcissism to practical, observable signs. This shift marks a transition from the "why" to the "how": how to spot narcissism in action and how to respond to it effectively.

CHAPTER 5:

The Telltale Signs

Picture this: You're drawn into the orbit of someone charismatic and charming, someone who makes you feel seen, heard, and valued like never before. At first, it's exhilarating—the attention, the intensity, the feeling of being special. But, gradually, the sheen starts to wear off. You find yourself second-guessing your thoughts, questioning your worth, and feeling perpetually off-balance. Welcome to the world where narcissistic tactics subtly shift the ground beneath you: a world where what starts as a dream can swiftly morph into a disorienting, challenging reality.

In the following sections, we will unravel the common tactics used in relationships by individuals with narcissistic tendencies. Through a blend of definitions, real-life scenarios, and expert insights, we will explore how these tactics work, their various types and stages, and, most importantly, the signs that can help you recognize them. This journey is not just about understanding these behaviors, but also about empowering you with the knowledge to navigate them effectively in your own life.

Ready to delve deeper into the telltale signs of narcissistic tactics? Let's begin.

Unveiling Narcissistic Tactics

Gaslighting: The Subtle Art of Altering Reality

Gaslighting is a form of psychological manipulation where the perpetrator, or gaslighter, seeks to sow doubt in the victim's mind, making them question their memory, perception, and even sanity. This tactic, when effectively employed, can erode the victim's sense of reality and self-trust, leading to significant emotional and psychological distress.

Understanding the Mechanics

Gaslighting unfolds in a manner that is often gradual and imperceptible at first. It begins with subtle manipulations, where the gaslighter might deny saying something they clearly did or question the victim's memory of an event. As time goes by, this behavior gradually intensifies, resulting in a recurring pattern where the victim's perception of reality is constantly eroded. The gaslighter may use tactics like outright denial, trivialization, or contradiction to disorient and control their victim.

Emma noticed her partner, Alex, frequently contradicted her recollections of past events. Whenever she brought up specific incidents, Alex would dismiss them, accusing her of misremembering or being overly sensitive. Gradually, Emma began to question her own memory and judgment, leading to a sense of confusion and self-doubt (National Domestic Violence Hotline, n.d.).

Recognizing the Signs and Stages of Gaslighting

We can identify gaslighting through several key signs:

- **Persistent Denial:** The gaslighter consistently denies their actions or words, even when confronted with evidence.

- **Distorting Facts:** They may twist information or events to align with their narrative, confusing the victim.

- **Belittling the Victim's Feelings:** The victim's emotions and experiences are minimized or ridiculed, often portrayed as an overreaction or delusion.

- **Inducing Isolation:** The victim's isolation from their support system makes them more dependent on the gaslighter.

Most times, the stages of gaslighting develop in the following progression:

1. **Disbelief:** Initially, the victim may dismiss the gaslighter's behavior as a simple misunderstanding.

2. **Defense:** As the behavior continues, the victim starts to defend their memory and perceptions, often feeling the need to prove their reality.

3. **Depression and Confusion:** Prolonged exposure to gaslighting can lead to feelings of hopelessness, confusion, and emotional exhaustion.

Navigating and Countering Gaslighting

Combating gaslighting involves recognizing the behavior and taking steps to reaffirm personal reality. It is important for victims to have faith in their experiences and seek external validation from trusted individuals, such as friends, family, or mental health professionals. Keeping a record of events and conversations can be an effective strategy to maintain a clear sense of reality. It's also important for victims to establish boundaries and assert their perspective in the face of gaslighting attempts (Ni, 2017).

Understanding gaslighting in depth lays the foundation for recognizing and resisting this manipulative tactic. As we continue exploring narcissistic behaviors, we'll next delve into the realm of guilt-tripping, another common strategy used in these complex dynamics.

Guilt-Tripping: The Manipulative Ploy for Control

Guilt-tripping is another prevalent tactic in the arsenal of narcissistic manipulation. This strategy involves inducing guilt in the victim to control or influence their behavior. By making the victim feel responsible for the narcissist's emotional well-being or failures, the narcissist exerts control and reaffirms their dominance in the relationship.

Mechanics of Guilt-Tripping

The essence of guilt-tripping lies in the manipulation of feelings of obligation and responsibility. Narcissists adept at this tactic often portray themselves as the victim or as suffering due to the actions or inactions of the victim. This can lead to the victim feeling overly responsible for the narcissist's happiness and well-being, often sacrificing their own needs in the process.

For instance, with Laura and Tom, Laura often found herself catering to Tom's needs and whims. Whenever she expressed a desire to spend time on her interests or with friends, Tom would lament how her actions made him feel neglected and unloved, effectively making Laura feel guilty for pursuing anything that didn't revolve around him (Raypole, 2020c).

Recognizing Guilt-Tripping in Action

The signs of guilt-tripping in a relationship can include

- **Emotional Coercion:** The narcissist may use emotional expressions like sadness or disappointment to manipulate the victim into compliance.

- **Victimhood:** They frequently portray themselves as the wronged party, shifting blame onto the victim.

- **Obligation:** The narcissist creates a sense of obligation, making the victim feel they owe them for past favors or sacrifices.

These tactics can significantly impact the victim's mental and emotional health, often leading to feelings of unwarranted guilt, anxiety, and a diminished sense of self-worth.

Counteracting Guilt-Tripping

To counteract guilt-tripping, it's important for victims to recognize these manipulative patterns and reaffirm their boundaries. This can involve questioning the legitimacy of the guilt imposed upon them and seeking external perspectives. Building a support network and engaging in self-care are crucial steps in mitigating the effects of guilt-tripping and regaining emotional autonomy.

Guilt-tripping, with its subtle emotional manipulation, can be challenging to detect and resist. However, understanding its dynamics is key to protecting oneself from this form of control in narcissistic relationships.

Triangulation: The Narcissist's Game of Divide and Conquer

Triangulation is a manipulative technique commonly employed that involves the use of a third party to create tension, sow discord, or validate the narcissist's perspective. By bringing a third person into the dynamics of the relationship, the narcissist can maintain control and keep their victims off-balance.

The Dynamics of Triangulation

In triangulation, the narcissist typically alternates between devaluing one person and elevating another. This not only creates rivalry and insecurity but also allows the narcissist to play the role of the sought-after individual. For example, in a workplace scenario, a narcissistic manager might pit two employees against each other, providing preferential treatment to one while criticizing the other. This creates a competitive environment where the employees vie for the manager's approval, inadvertently reinforcing the manager's perceived importance.

Another form of triangulation is using a third party to communicate with the victim, rather than speaking directly. This indirect communication can be confusing and frustrating for the victim, as it creates a sense of distance and distortion in the relationship.

Recognizing Signs of Triangulation

Signs that triangulation is occurring include

- **Feeling Pitted Against Others:** The victim feels as if they are in competition with others for the narcissist's attention or approval.

- **Conflicting Messages:** Receiving different messages from the narcissist and the third party, leading to confusion and uncertainty.

- **Feeling Isolated:** The victim feels isolated or excluded due to the narcissist's interactions with the third party.

Strategies to Counteract Triangulation

Dealing with triangulation requires recognizing the tactic and refusing to participate in the game. Victims should strive to maintain direct communication and avoid getting drawn into comparisons or competitions set up by the narcissist. Seeking support from trusted friends or a therapist can provide clarity and validation, helping the victim to stay grounded in their perception of reality.

Triangulation, with its potential to create emotional turmoil and instability, is a powerful tool in the narcissist's repertoire. Understanding this tactic is essential for anyone involved in a relationship with a narcissist, as it empowers them to recognize and resist manipulation.

Projection: The Narcissist's Defense Mechanism

Projection is a psychological defense mechanism widely used in narcissistic relationships. It involves the narcissist attributing their own undesirable feelings, thoughts, or traits to another person. By projecting these aspects onto others, the narcissist deflects blame and maintains their self-image of perfection.

Understanding Projection in Narcissistic Dynamics

Projection in narcissism occurs when individuals refuse to acknowledge their own negative qualities and instead attribute these qualities to others. This can manifest in various ways, such as a narcissist accusing someone else of being selfish, manipulative, or even narcissistic, which are actually traits of the narcissists themselves.

An illustrative example is the case of Helen and Mark. Helen, who often manipulated situations to her advantage, regularly accused Mark of being deceitful and manipulative. In reality, these accusations were a projection of her behaviors and traits, shifting the focus away from her actions and onto Mark (Peterson, 2023).

Identifying Projection in Relationships

Key indicators of projection include

- **Accusations:** The narcissist makes frequent accusations that seem to describe their behavior more than the accused's.

- **Denial:** When confronted with their actions, the narcissist vehemently denies wrongdoing and instead redirects the blame.

- **Pattern of Blame:** There's a consistent pattern where the narcissist shifts responsibility for their faults onto others.

This mechanism not only serves as a tool for blame-shifting but also confuses and destabilizes the victim, often leading to self-doubt and a skewed perception of reality.

Navigating and Responding to Projection

Addressing projection involves recognizing the tactic and understanding its purpose in the narcissist's arsenal. Victims are encouraged to maintain a clear sense of reality, avoiding internalizing the narcissist's projections. Setting firm boundaries and seeking external validation can help in maintaining an objective perspective on the situation.

Projection, while a common defense mechanism, can have significant implications in relationships, especially when employed by individuals with narcissistic tendencies. Recognizing and understanding this tactic is crucial in navigating and protecting oneself from the psychological effects of being in a relationship with a narcissist.

Love Bombing: The Narcissist's Intense Courtship Ritual

Love bombing is a manipulative strategy frequently started at the beginning of relationships by individuals with narcissistic traits. Characterized by excessive attention, flattery, and affection, love bombing is designed to quickly win over and control the victim. This tactic creates a powerful emotional bond, making it difficult for the victim to see the narcissist's true intentions.

Exploring the Mechanics of Love Bombing

The process of love bombing involves showering the victim with praise, gifts, and grand gestures. This intense courtship is often disproportionate to the length and depth of the relationship, creating a whirlwind romance. The aim is to sweep the victim off their feet, making them emotionally dependent on the narcissist.

For instance, Sarah experienced love bombing when she started dating Michael. He was incredibly attentive, constantly sending flowers, planning extravagant dates, and expressing his affection in grandiose terms. This overwhelming attention initially made Sarah feel special and loved, but she soon began to feel smothered and controlled as Michael's behavior became increasingly demanding and possessive (Corelli, 2023b).

Signs and Consequences of Love Bombing

There are several signs that can help in identifying love bombing.

- **Rapid Pace of the Relationship:** The relationship progresses quickly, with the narcissist pushing for commitment early on.

- **Overwhelming Attention and Gifts:** The narcissist bombards the victim with attention, compliments, and gifts, often excessively.

- **Emotional Intensity:** The relationship is marked by an intense emotional bond that feels overwhelming and uneven.

While initially flattering, love bombing can lead to an unhealthy power dynamic, where the victim becomes emotionally dependent on the narcissist. This dependency sets the stage for future manipulation and control within the relationship.

Countering Love Bombing

Recognizing love bombing early in a relationship is crucial. It's important to maintain personal boundaries and take the time to genuinely get to know the other person. Keeping a level of independence, such as maintaining hobbies and connections with friends and family, can provide a balanced perspective on the relationship.

Understanding love bombing allows individuals to approach new relationships with caution, particularly when they encounter overwhelming attention and affection that seem disproportionate or premature.

Smear Campaign: The Narcissist's Strategy of Defamation

The smear campaign is a manipulative tactic employed by narcissists to discredit, defame, or isolate their victims. It involves spreading false or exaggerated information about the victim, often to maintain control, punish, or simply out of spite. Understanding how smear campaigns operate is crucial for those entangled in the manipulative webs of narcissists.

Unraveling the Dynamics of Smear Campaigns

In a smear campaign, the narcissist systematically spreads malicious rumors or accusations about their victim. This tactic is often used when the victim challenges or leaves the narcissist, triggering a vindictive response. The narcissist's goal is to damage the victim's reputation, relationships, and credibility, thereby keeping the upper hand.

Jessica's decision to end her relationship with her narcissistic partner David is an example of a smear campaign. In retaliation, David began spreading rumors about Jessica among their mutual friends, painting her as unfaithful and unstable. These rumors not only strained Jessica's friendships but also made her question her decision and her own sanity (Stines, 2017).

Recognizing the Signs of a Smear Campaign

Signs that a smear campaign is underway include

- **Sudden Change in Social Dynamics:** Friends and acquaintances may begin to act differently around the victim, showing they might have heard negative rumors.

- **Direct Accusations:** The victim may hear directly from others about the accusations or rumors being spread by the narcissist.

- **Isolation:** The victim might find themselves increasingly isolated as their social circle shrinks because of the spread of misinformation.

Navigating Through a Smear Campaign

Dealing with a smear campaign involves staying grounded in one's truth and avoiding direct confrontation with the narcissist, which can escalate the situation. Maintaining open communication with close friends and family and seeking support from a therapist can be crucial in navigating this challenging situation. It's also important to document any instances of defamation for potential legal recourse.

Smear campaigns, with their potential to cause significant emotional and reputational damage, are a harmful tactic used by narcissists. Understanding this tactic and knowing how to respond is essential for anyone who finds themselves targeted in such a situation.

Playing the Victim: The Narcissist's Tactical Reversal

In the intricate dance of narcissistic manipulation, "playing the victim" is a common tactic. This strategy involves the narcissist portraying themselves as the injured party, regardless of the actual circumstances. By assuming the role of the victim, the narcissist seeks to garner sympathy, evade responsibility, and manipulate those around them.

The Art of Victimhood in Narcissistic Relationships

Narcissists, adept at playing the victim, skillfully turn the tables, often in situations where they are actually the perpetrator or at fault. This tactic serves multiple purposes: It deflects attention away from their misdeeds, elicits sympathy, and often positions the true victim in a defensive stance.

For example, in the dynamic between Linda and her partner, George, who exhibited narcissistic traits, George frequently twisted situations. When confronted about his hurtful behavior, he would turn the narrative around, claiming he was the one being mistreated or misunderstood. This reversal often left Linda feeling guilty and questioning her own actions, despite her initial intent to address a legitimate concern.

Identifying the "Victim Play"

Key indicators that a narcissist is playing the victim include

- **Shifting Blame:** The narcissist deflects blame for their actions onto others, often the actual victim.

- **Seeking Sympathy:** They elicit sympathy from others, portraying themselves as unfairly treated or targeted.

- **Contradicting Evidence:** Despite evidence to the contrary, the narcissist maintains their victim narrative.

Countermeasures Against the Victim Tactic

Navigating this manipulation requires a clear understanding of the situation and firm boundaries. Recognizing the tactic is the first step; it's crucial not to get drawn into the false narrative. Maintaining a factual account of events and avoiding emotional entanglement in the narcissist's story can help in staying grounded. It's also beneficial to seek external perspectives to validate the reality of the situation.

This knowledge empowers individuals to respond appropriately and protect themselves from being drawn into the narcissist's distorted reality.

Hoovering: The Narcissist's Tactic of Reentanglement

Hoovering, named after the famous vacuum cleaner brand, is a manipulation tactic used by narcissists to "suck" their victims back into a relationship or interaction after a period of separation or the end of a relationship. This tactic is frequently used by the narcissist when they perceive their power over the victim diminishing, causing confusion and harm to the receiving end.

The Cycle of Hoovering in Narcissistic Dynamics

Hoovering usually occurs after there has been a break in the relationship, whether initiated by the victim or due to the narcissist's behavior. The narcissist may reach out with seemingly genuine apologies, promises to change, or attempts to rekindle the romance. These gestures, however, are typically superficial and serve the narcissist's need to regain control, not a sincere desire for reconciliation or improvement.

Consider the scenario involving Maria and her ex-partner, Eric. After a tumultuous relationship, Maria ended things. A few weeks later, Eric began reaching out with messages expressing regret, professing his love, and promising he had changed. Initially, Maria felt confused and conflicted, as the gestures tugged at her desire for the relationship to have worked.

Identifying Signs of Hoovering

If you're wondering whether someone is hoovering, keep an eye out for these key signs:

- **Unexpected Contact:** The narcissist reaches out unexpectedly after a period of no communication, often with sentimental messages.

- **Promises of Change:** The narcissist makes promises to change behaviors that were problematic in the relationship.

- **Playing on Emotions:** The narcissist may use guilt, nostalgia, or emotional pleas to appeal to the victim's sympathies and feelings.

Strategies to Resist Hoovering

Dealing with hoovering effectively involves recognizing the tactic and understanding its purpose. It's essential to maintain boundaries set after the relationship ends and to resist the temptation to engage with these attempts. Reminding oneself of the reasons for the relationship's end and seeking support from trusted friends or a therapist can provide strength and clarity during this challenging time.

Hoovering is a common strategy used by narcissists to maintain or regain control of relationships. Being aware of this tactic enables individuals to make informed decisions about their interactions with the narcissist and to protect their emotional well-being.

Flying Monkeys: The Narcissist's Unwitting Accomplices

In the realm of narcissistic manipulation, the term "flying monkeys" describes individuals who, often unknowingly, are manipulated into serving the narcissist's agenda. Borrowed from the imagery of the winged creatures in *The Wizard of Oz*, this concept illustrates how narcissists enlist others to do their bidding, furthering their control and manipulation.

The Role of Flying Monkeys in Narcissistic Manipulation

Flying monkeys are typically friends, family members, or even colleagues who are drawn into the narcissist's manipulative dynamics. They might be fed misinformation or partial truths, leading them to support the narcissist's narrative. These individuals often become tools in the narcissist's arsenal, used to spread rumors, ostracize the victim, or gather information.

Alice's story shows how she ended up isolated from her friend group after breaking up with her narcissistic partner, Dan. Unbeknownst to Alice, Dan had been telling their mutual friends Alice was the one who had been abusive and controlling in the relationship, leading the friends to side with him and distance themselves from Alice.

Recognizing the Involvement of Flying Monkeys

Indications that flying monkeys are at play include

- **Shifts in Social Dynamics:** Changes in the behavior of friends or colleagues that align with the narcissist's narrative.

- **Indirect Communication:** Messages or accusations from the narcissist are relayed through mutual acquaintances.

- **Increased Gossip or Rumors:** An uptick in gossip or rumors that trace back to the narcissist.

Dealing With Flying Monkeys

Navigating the involvement of flying monkeys requires a careful approach. It's important to avoid engaging in the drama and to maintain a clear understanding of the situation. Open and honest communication with mutual acquaintances can sometimes clarify misunderstandings. However, it's also crucial to recognize when to step back and prioritize one's mental health over trying to correct every misconception.

This concept highlights the extent of a narcissist's influence and manipulation, often extending beyond direct interactions with the victim. By understanding this tactic, individuals can better protect themselves from the broader impacts of narcissistic manipulation.

The Labyrinth of Narcissistic Manipulation: Navigating Revenge Seeking

Revenge seeking within narcissistic relationships is a complex and often alarming behavior. It emerges primarily when narcissists perceive an affront to their ego or authority. Unlike typical responses to perceived wrongs, narcissistic revenge seeking is driven by a deep-seated need for control and a desire to assert dominance. This behavior can manifest in various forms, ranging from subtle passive aggression to overt acts of retaliation.

Decoding the Narcissist's Revenge Mindset

Narcissists often view any criticism or challenge as a personal attack, triggering an intense and disproportionate need for retribution. Their revenge is not simply about evening the score; it's an attempt to restore their sense of superiority and control. The narcissist's tactics may include spreading rumors, sabotaging the victim's professional or personal life, or engaging in legal warfare.

An illustrative case is that of Kevin, whose decision to leave his narcissistic business partner, Robert, led to a vindictive response. Robert not only launched a smear campaign against Kevin, attempting to tarnish his professional reputation but also engaged in legal tactics designed to drain Kevin's resources and energy.

Spotting the Signs of Narcissistic Revenge

Recognizing the signs of a narcissist's revenge seeking can be critical in mitigating its impact. Key indicators include

- **Aggressive Retaliation:** The narcissist may engage in overt actions intended to harm or undermine the victim.

- **Subtle Sabotage:** More covert actions, like spreading rumors or influencing others against the victim, are common.

- **Persistent Vindictiveness:** Unlike a one-time response to conflict, narcissistic revenge tends to be ongoing and relentless.

Coping With Narcissistic Revenge

Dealing with a revenge-seeking narcissist involves a strategic and often cautious approach. It's crucial to avoid direct confrontation, which may escalate the situation. Instead, focus on safeguarding one's reputation and well-being, possibly seeking legal counsel in extreme cases. Building a strong support network and documenting any hostile actions can also be important defensive measures.

DARVO: The Narcissist's Twisted Defense Strategy

DARVO, an acronym for Deny, Attack, Reverse Victim, and Offender, is a manipulative defense strategy often used by narcissists when accused of wrongdoing. This tactic serves to deflect blame, obscure the truth, and maintain the narcissist's facade of innocence. Understanding DARVO is essential for those dealing with narcissistic individuals, as it reveals the complex methods they use to evade accountability and manipulate perceptions.

The Mechanics of DARVO in Action

DARVO begins with an outright denial of any wrongdoing, followed by a counterattack against the accuser, and culminates in portraying oneself as the victim, thereby reversing the roles of victim and offender. This tactic not only confuses the accuser but also garners sympathy and support for the narcissist from others.

Consider the scenario involving Janet and her partner, Carl, who displayed narcissistic tendencies. When Janet confronted Carl about his infidelity, he initially denied the allegations (Deny), then accused her of being overly suspicious and jealous (Attack), and finally claimed that her accusations were causing him emotional distress, portraying himself as the aggrieved party (Reverse Victim and Offender).

Recognizing the Signs of DARVO

Signs that a narcissist is employing DARVO include

- **Denial of Accountability:** The narcissist vehemently denies any wrongdoing, regardless of evidence.

- **Counterattacks:** The narcissist deflects by attacking the accuser's character, motives, or behavior.

- **Victim Stance:** The narcissist reframes the situation to appear as the wronged party, often eliciting sympathy from others.

Responding to DARVO

Dealing with DARVO requires a clear understanding of the tactic and a firm commitment to reality. It's important not to be drawn into the narcissist's narrative or become defensive. Staying grounded in the facts and seeking external support can help maintain perspective. Documenting interactions can also be useful, especially in situations where legal or professional implications are involved.

DARVO is a sophisticated form of psychological manipulation used by narcissists to escape blame and manipulate their environment.

Emotional Blackmail: The Narcissist's Coercive Control

Emotional blackmail is a manipulative technique often used by narcissists to exert control over their victims through guilt, fear, and obligation. This tactic is insidious, as it exploits the victim's emotional vulnerabilities, coercing them into compliance with the narcissist's demands. Understanding emotional blackmail is crucial for anyone entangled in a relationship with a narcissist, as it sheds light on the coercive tactics used to manipulate and maintain power.

Navigating the Treacherous Waters of Emotional Blackmail

Emotional blackmail typically involves the narcissist threatening to inflict emotional pain or withhold affection if the victim does not comply with their wishes. This can take many forms, from subtle hints and passive-aggressive comments to outright threats and ultimatums. The underlying goal is to manipulate the victim into feeling guilty or anxious about not meeting the narcissist's needs or expectations.

Consider the experience of Jason, whose partner, a narcissist, frequently used emotional blackmail to control him. Whenever he made plans that did not include his partner, she would react with extreme sadness or anger, suggesting that he didn't care about her or their relationship. This would leave Jason feeling guilty and often lead him to cancel his plans to appease her.

Recognizing the Patterns of Emotional Blackmail

Key indicators of emotional blackmail include

- **Threats of Withdrawal:** The narcissist may threaten to withdraw love and support or even end the relationship if their demands are not met.

- **Guilt-Tripping:** The victim is made to feel guilty for not acquiescing to the narcissist's wishes.

- **Fear Tactics:** The narcissist instills fear by suggesting negative consequences if the victim does not comply.

Strategies to Counter Emotional Blackmail

Countering emotional blackmail requires recognizing the tactic and understanding its purpose. Victims should strive to maintain their boundaries and not give in to the manipulation. It's important to recognize that complying with the narcissist's demands only reinforces the behavior. Seeking support from friends, family, or a therapist can provide the perspective and strength to deal with emotional blackmail effectively.

Emerging From the Shadows: Empowering Steps Beyond Narcissistic Manipulation

Reflecting on the insights we've garnered in our exploration of narcissistic manipulation, we find ourselves at a pivotal juncture. This exploration has been more than just an academic exercise; it has been a journey into the heart of human relationships, where the line between affection and manipulation often blurs. We've dissected complex behaviors, understanding how narcissists weave their tapestry of control through tactics like gaslighting, love bombing, and smear campaigns. Each of these methods, intricate in its design, reveals the depths to which manipulation can permeate the fabric of relationships.

The real-life scenarios we've delved into have not just been stories; they've been windows into the experiences of those entangled in the web of narcissistic manipulation. These narratives have brought to life the subtle, often invisible threads of control and influence that narcissists exert. They've shown us how the weight of these manipulations can press down on the psyche, leaving individuals questioning their reality, their worth, and their ability to discern truth from fabrication.

In unpacking these tactics, we've uncovered more than just the mechanisms of manipulation; we've tapped into a wellspring of understanding and empathy. This knowledge arms us, not with weapons, but with shields: shields of awareness, discernment, and self-assurance. It's this understanding that turns the tables, transforming victims into survivors, and survivors into advocates of their own well-being.

As we transition from this revelation of tactics, our path leads us toward a terrain of empowerment and resilience. The journey ahead is about transforming knowledge into power: the power to recognize, resist, and recover. It's about building fortresses of self-esteem and moats of boundaries to protect our emotional well-being. It's about learning to navigate the stormy seas of manipulation with the compass of insight and the anchor of self-respect.

This next phase in our journey is more than just a continuation; it's a shift from defense to offense, from understanding to action, from being acted upon to taking charge. It's about charting a course through the turbulent waters of manipulation and emerging not just unscathed but stronger, wiser, and more empowered.

As we embark on this new chapter, we carry with us the lessons learned, the insights gained, and the stories that have touched our hearts. With these tools in hand, we're not just moving forward; we're ascending to a new level of personal empowerment and relational understanding. Let's step into this new phase together, ready to turn our knowledge into a shield and our experiences into stepping stones toward a more empowered and self-aware future.

CHAPTER 6:

Gaining Ground

In the soft glow of the evening, Anna found herself yet again in the same old armchair across from Michael. The room, with its faded wallpaper and the clock ticking monotonously, felt like a stage set for their recurring drama. Their conversations, once filled with laughter and dreams, had turned into a cyclic dance of accusations and rebuttals, a tiring routine that left Anna feeling drained and lost.

As Michael spoke, his words were a familiar melody of charm and persuasion laced with subtle jabs and manipulations. He was a master of words, turning every argument around, making Anna question her own memory, her feelings, and her sanity. She remembered the first time she had found herself in this situation; how bewildered and alone she had felt. Back then, she had believed in the promises of change, the heartfelt apologies, and the fleeting moments of affection. But, as the cycle repeated, those promises faded into the background, overshadowed by a relentless pattern of control and emotional turmoil.

Anna's mind wandered to their early days: the whirlwind romance that had swept her off her feet. Michael had been charming, attentive, and seemingly everything she had ever wanted. But, as the months passed, the red flags that she had initially dismissed as quirks began to form a daunting pattern. His sweet words turned into criticisms, the caring gestures became controlling demands, and the apologies turned into accusations. Every time she tried to break free, Michael would reappear with grand gestures and persuasive words, pulling her back into the vortex of their toxic relationship.

Yet here she was again, listening to the same excuses, feeling the same old knot of anxiety in her stomach. She realized that understanding

Michael's behavior was not enough; what she needed were effective strategies to break this cycle, reclaim her sense of self, and navigate away from the emotional maze she was trapped in.

Anna's journey to untangle herself from the web of her tumultuous relationship with Michael led her to a deeper understanding of the narcissistic abuse cycle. This cycle, a psychological trap laid out in a series of predictable stages, is often hard to recognize from within, but understanding it is crucial for those seeking to break free from its grasp.

Dissecting the Narcissistic Abuse Cycle

The cycle typically begins with the idealization stage, where the narcissist, like a chameleon, presents an alluring and flawless facade. They shower their partner with praise, attention, and affection, creating a mirage of a perfect relationship. This stage is about building a dependency; the victim, bathed in this seemingly unconditional love, finds themselves deeply attached. Anna recalled the early days with Michael, filled with grand gestures and passionate declarations, a stark contrast to what followed (Gupta, 2022).

As the relationship progresses, it morphs into the devaluation phase. Here, the narcissist's mask begins to slip, revealing a more sinister face. Criticism and contempt replace compliments, and emotional withdrawal supersedes affection. Anna experienced this shift firsthand, as Michael's demeanor changed from caring to critical, leaving her feeling confused and inadequate.

The final stage is the discard step, where the narcissist abandons their partner, leaving a trail of emotional devastation. This phase often results in the victim feeling worthless and isolated. However, it's not uncommon for the narcissists to return to the idealization phase, restarting the cycle and trapping their partner in a continuous loop of emotional turbulence.

Breaking Free

Anna's realization of the narcissistic abuse cycle became a pivotal moment in her journey toward emotional liberation. As she pieced together the stages of idealization, devaluation, and discard, a clear picture emerged of the manipulative pattern she had been ensnared in with Michael. This understanding was both a jolt of harsh reality and a beacon of hope: a signal that while she had been trapped, there was a path to freedom.

In recognizing these cycles, Anna saw Michael's actions not as reflections of her worth, but as manifestations of his own troubled psyche. This shift in perspective was empowering. It helped her understand that the intense highs and devastating lows of their relationship were not a testament to passionate love but indicators of a deeply unhealthy dynamic.

The final stage of discard, which had once left her feeling abandoned and worthless, now stood as a crucial juncture. It was no longer just an end but an opportunity: a chance to step out of the cycle and reclaim her agency. Anna established boundaries where there had been none and sought support from friends, family, and professionals, each step taking her further away from the turmoil and closer to a newfound sense of self.

Anna's story, much like Emily's experience with Jake, serves as a testament to the resilience and strength that can emerge when confronting the realities of a relationship marred by narcissistic abuse. For Anna, understanding the narcissistic abuse cycle was not just about coming to terms with her past, but about charting a course for a healthier, more empowered future.

With this newfound knowledge and resolve, we turn our focus to actionable strategies and insights. These tools will not only aid in recognizing narcissistic behavior but also provide practical ways to effectively deal with it, marking a transition from understanding to action, from victimhood to empowerment.

What "Not" to Do With Narcissists

In the intricate dance of interaction with narcissists, it's not just what you do, but also what you avoid doing that counts. Managing complex relationships requires both proactive strategies and awareness of potential missteps.

The first key to navigating these treacherous waters is to minimize emotional reactivity. Narcissists often seek to elicit strong emotional responses; they thrive on the turmoil they create. Keeping a level head by responding with calmness rather than anger or frustration can be disarming. It's a tactic that not only preserves your emotional energy but also denies the narcissist the reaction they seek. For example, in a workplace scenario, when a narcissistic colleague attempts to provoke you with underhanded comments, choosing a composed response over an emotional outburst can be a powerful countermeasure.

Understanding that a narcissist's behavior is more about their own internal struggles than anything about you is another crucial aspect. It's a reflection of their issues, not a measure of your worth. This perspective is essential in maintaining your self-esteem and not internalizing the negative behavior directed at you. Consider a family gathering where a narcissistic relative constantly belittles your achievements. Recognizing that these comments stem from the narcissist's insecurities, not your inadequacies, helps in maintaining your sense of self-worth.

Resisting the urge to change or "fix" a narcissist is also important. This often futile endeavor can drain your emotional resources. Narcissism is a deep-rooted personality issue and believing that your efforts will bring about change can result in disappointment and frustration. Instead, focusing on how you respond and setting boundaries can be more effective.

Remember that navigating life with a narcissist, be it at work, home, or in social settings, requires a balanced approach of strategic engagement and mindful avoidance. By understanding and implementing what not to do, you can safeguard your emotional well-being and navigate these challenging relationships with greater confidence and control.

As we move forward, the focus will shift to specific strategies and practical tips for dealing with various behaviors exhibited by narcissists. These insights aim to equip you with a toolkit for managing and mitigating the impact of narcissistic manipulation in your life.

What Should You Do?

It's clear that taking a reactive approach is ineffective when dealing with narcissistic individuals. A more intentional and proactive strategy is needed due to the unpredictable and volatile nature of these interactions. Understanding the intricacies of narcissistic behavior is only the first step; real empowerment comes from applying this knowledge in practical, real-world situations.

Narcissists, with their penchant for manipulation and control, often create environments of confusion and emotional upheaval. Without a cohesive plan, we can end up constantly on the defensive, trapped in a cycle of reactive responses that have minimal impact on the relationship's dynamics. By adopting a proactive approach, we can shift from being a passive participant to an empowered actor, capable of influencing the direction and nature of these interactions.

This empowerment is multifaceted. It's not just about avoiding harm or diffusing tense situations; it's about reclaiming agency within relationships that have historically been imbalanced. The focus is on setting boundaries, asserting needs, and preserving emotional well-being. Armed with the right strategies, individuals can effectively counter manipulative tactics, reduce the emotional toll of these interactions, and create a sense of stability and predictability in environments that are often anything but.

Dealing with narcissistic behavior is both challenging and rewarding. By moving from understanding to action, from passive to proactive, we empower ourselves not just to survive these interactions but to thrive within them. Let's embark on this path of empowerment together, exploring the proactive strategies that can transform our approach to dealing with narcissistic behavior.

Responding to Gaslighting

Responding to gaslighting requires a careful and self-affirming approach. When you're amid such manipulation, it can feel like you're losing your grip on what's true and what's not. The key to countering this unsettling experience lies in building a foundation of trust in your own experiences and perceptions.

Start by creating a personal record of events and interactions. This can be as simple as jotting down notes in a journal or keeping a file on your phone. When a situation arises where your memory or perception is challenged, refer to these notes. They serve as tangible reminders of what actually transpired, providing a grounding anchor in moments of doubt. This practice not only reaffirms your reality but also bolsters your confidence in your memory and judgment.

It's crucial to seek validation outside of the gaslighting context. Confiding in trusted friends, family members, or a therapist can offer an external perspective that counters the distortion created by the narcissist. These supportive relationships are invaluable, providing a reality check and reinforcing that your experiences and feelings are valid and acknowledged.

Remember, the goal in responding to gaslighting isn't to prove the narcissist wrong or to change their behavior—that might be an impossible task—but to preserve your sense of self and reality. By building this self-trust and seeking external validation, you create a protective barrier against the destabilizing effects of gaslighting, empowering yourself to navigate these interactions with greater clarity and confidence.

Handling Guilt Trips

When you're on the receiving end of a guilt trip, it can feel like being caught in a web of obligation and remorse, often for things beyond your control or responsibility. The key to navigating this tactic is to recognize it for what it is: a manipulation tool, not a reflection of your character or intentions.

First, it's essential to internally acknowledge and affirm your own feelings and needs. When a narcissist attempts to guilt-trip you, take a moment to reflect on the situation. Ask yourself: Is this guilt mine to carry? Am I being blamed unfairly? This self-reflection can help you distinguish between legitimate remorse and imposed guilt.

Once you've identified a guilt trip, communicate your boundaries clearly and calmly. For instance, if a narcissistic individual accuses you of not caring enough because you set aside time for yourself, respond with a firm yet composed statement like, "I understand you're upset, but it's also important for me to take care of my needs." Such a response acknowledges their feelings without succumbing to the guilt they're trying to impose.

It's also beneficial to practice not internalizing the guilt. Narcissists are adept at making others feel responsible for their emotions or situations.

Reminding yourself that you're not responsible for their happiness or satisfaction is crucial in these moments.

In handling guilt trips, the aim is not to confront the narcissist or change their behavior—which is often a futile effort—but to protect your own emotional well-being. By recognizing the tactic, reaffirming your needs, and communicating your boundaries, you empower yourself to respond to guilt trips in a way that maintains your emotional health and respects your personal boundaries.

Dealing With Projection

Experiencing projection can be disorienting and hurtful, as you may be accused of behaviors and attitudes that do not reflect your true nature. The challenge lies in distinguishing between the narcissist's distorted accusations and your actual self.

One effective approach is to maintain a clear understanding of your own actions and character. When faced with projection, it's easy to get caught up in defending yourself or trying to disprove the narcissist's claims. However, a more productive strategy is to internally reaffirm your understanding of yourself. Reflect on your actions and intentions, and remind yourself of your true nature, which stands in contrast to the traits being projected onto you.

Responding to projection involves a careful balance between addressing the behavior and not absorbing the negative traits attributed to you. If a narcissist accuses you of selfishness when you set boundaries, calmly state your perspective without accepting their projected trait. A response like, "I understand that you're upset, but setting boundaries is important for my well-being," acknowledges their feelings without internalizing the false accusation.

It's also important to recognize that projection is more about the narcissist's internal conflicts than it is about you. Their accusations are often reflections of their own issues, insecurities, or behaviors.

Understanding this can help you maintain emotional distance and not take their projections personally.

To effectively deal with projection, we must remain confident in our self-knowledge and respond with integrity. It involves knowing when to engage and when to step back, ensuring that you don't get entangled in the narcissist's distorted reality.

Navigating Triangulation

Triangulation can create unnecessary drama and conflict, often leaving you feeling confused, isolated, or pitted against someone else. The key to effectively handling this tactic is to recognize it when it happens and to maintain direct and clear communication with all parties involved.

When you suspect you're being triangulated, the first step is to step back and assess the situation objectively. Reflect on whether the third party's involvement is necessary or beneficial. Triangulation is a go-to strategy for narcissists to control and manipulate situations by forming alliances or creating discord. Identifying this is crucial in formulating an effective response.

To address triangulation, it is best to communicate directly with the parties involved. This might mean having an honest conversation with the third party to clarify any misunderstandings or misconceptions. For example, if a narcissistic individual is using a friend or colleague to relay messages or to create a rivalry, approach that person directly to discuss the situation. This direct approach can help diffuse the tension and remove the power from the narcissist's manipulative strategy.

It's also important to set boundaries around communication and relationships. Politely express your preference for handling issues directly without involving others unnecessarily. For instance, you might say, "I feel more comfortable discussing these matters directly with you, rather than involving [third party]. Let's keep our communication between us."

The objective when dealing with triangulation is to avoid playing into their game and detach yourself from the manipulative triangle they are attempting to form. By maintaining open communication and setting boundaries, you can effectively navigate triangulation, reducing the confusion and conflict it typically brings into relationships.

Countering Love Bombing

Love bombing can be deceptive, making it seem like you are receiving genuine affection and interest. However, its intensity is often a disguise for manipulation and control. Recognizing love bombing for what it truly is serves as the first step in countering its effects.

One effective strategy is to maintain a healthy pace in the relationship. Narcissists using love bombing often rush intimacy and commitment. It's important to slow things down and take time to really get to know the person. This allows you to assess the relationship more objectively and to recognize any red flags that might emerge.

Maintaining your independence is also crucial when dealing with love bombing. Narcissists often use this tactic to make their targets dependent on them for emotional fulfillment. By ensuring you have a life outside of the relationship—spending time with friends, pursuing hobbies, and maintaining your routines—you can keep a sense of self that is separate from the relationship.

Setting boundaries is another key step. Be clear about what is acceptable and what isn't in terms of the pace of the relationship, the time spent together, and how you expect to be treated. Communicating these boundaries clearly to the narcissist can help prevent them from overstepping and can give you control over how the relationship progresses.

Last, trust your guts. If you feel that the relationship is moving too fast, or if the attention feels overwhelming or insincere, pay attention to these feelings. Trusting your intuition can help you navigate the situation effectively and make decisions that are in your best interest.

Countering love bombing is not about rejecting affection, but about recognizing and responding to manipulation. To avoid being caught in the trap of love bombing, take it slow, stay independent, set boundaries, and trust your instincts.

Addressing Smear Campaigns

When you find yourself the target of a smear campaign, it can feel like you're battling against an overwhelming tide of misinformation and character assassination. The key to effectively addressing this tactic is to maintain your composure and to adopt a proactive stance in safeguarding your reputation.

The first step is to avoid reacting impulsively. Narcissists start these campaigns to provoke a response, often hoping to portray you as unstable or unreasonable. By responding in a calm and measured manner, you deny them this victory. It's crucial to assess the situation carefully and plan your response, rather than reacting out of hurt or anger.

One effective way to counter a smear campaign is through open and honest communication with those affected or involved. This might involve discussing the situation with your friends, family, or colleagues to clarify any misconceptions and to present your side of the story. It's important, however, to avoid getting into a mudslinging match with the narcissist. Focus instead on presenting your perspective in a straightforward and dignified manner.

Another crucial tool is to lean on your support system. Dealing with character attacks can be emotionally draining and isolating, making the support of friends, family, or a counselor invaluable. They can provide not only emotional support but also a grounded perspective on the situation.

Finally, it's important to continue to conduct yourself with integrity. Your actions and behavior can often be the best counter to a smear campaign. By continuing to be the person you know you are, you show those around you the untruths in the narcissist's narrative.

Navigating a smear campaign is challenging, but with a composed and proactive approach, you can mitigate its impact. Remember, the objective is not to defeat the narcissists at their own game but to protect your own integrity and well-being.

Coping With Playing the Victim

Dealing with a narcissist who plays the victim is complicated—you have to get their game and establish strong boundaries. When faced with this behavior, it's crucial to differentiate between genuine victimhood and manipulative theatrics.

One key aspect of dealing with this tactic is to maintain a clear perspective on the situation. Narcissists adept at playing the victim can be convincing, often stirring up feelings of guilt or pity. It's important to assess the situation objectively and remind yourself of the broader context of the narcissist's behavior. Look at the patterns rather than isolated incidents—does this portrayal align with their overall behavior and past actions?

Another important strategy is to avoid getting emotionally entangled in their narrative. While it's natural to feel empathy, it's crucial to protect yourself from being manipulated by these emotional appeals. Offering support or solutions is fine, but be wary of being drawn into a cycle of rescuing or enabling their behavior.

Communicating your observations and boundaries assertively can also be effective. If you feel the narcissist is using their victim status to manipulate or control you, express your perspective calmly and clearly. For instance, you might say, "I can see that you're upset, but I feel this issue is being used to shift focus from the actual problem."

Sometimes, having a third party's perspective can help in validating your experiences and providing guidance on how to proceed.

Ultimately, coping with a narcissist playing the victim is about balancing empathy with self-protection. By doing this, you can navigate tough interactions while taking care of yourself and respecting your limits.

Handling Hoovering

When narcissists feel like they're losing control or not getting what they want, they often start hoovering. They'll reach out acting like they want to make up, show interest again, or act like they urgently need your support.

The first and most crucial step is to recognize it for what it is—an attempt to manipulate you back into a dynamic that is likely unhealthy. It's important to remember the reasons why you distanced yourself in the first place. Reflect on the patterns of the relationship and the impact it had on your well-being. This reflection can reinforce your decision to maintain distance.

Reaffirming your boundaries is key. This might mean not responding to calls or messages, or clearly stating that you are no longer available in the same capacity as before. Let's say your narcissistic ex tries to get back together, promising they've changed. You could respond with a polite but firm message, letting them know you've moved on and wishing them the best.

It's also important to prepare yourself emotionally for these attempts. Narcissists can be very persuasive, tapping into your vulnerabilities and emotional triggers. Strengthening your support network and possibly seeking professional guidance can provide you with the emotional backing you need to stay strong in your resolve.

Sometimes, complete disengagement might be necessary. This could involve blocking phone numbers or social media connections, or changing your routine to avoid encounters. Taking these steps can be challenging, especially if there are lingering emotions, but they are sometimes necessary to protect your emotional and psychological health.

Handling hoovering is ultimately about valuing your well-being and staying true to the progress you've made since distancing yourself from the narcissistic individual.

Responding to Flying Monkeys

Managing interactions with flying monkeys requires a blend of tact, direct communication, and a strong sense of personal boundaries.

The first step is to identify the dynamic. Understand that these individuals may be acting under the influence of manipulation, possibly without full awareness of the situation's complexity. They might be friends, family members, or colleagues who have been fed a distorted version of events or who are trying to mediate without knowing the full story.

Direct communication is key. If someone in this role approaches you, handle the situation with openness and honesty. For example, if a mutual friend relays a message from a narcissist or attempts to mediate a reconciliation, it might be necessary to clarify your stance and the reasons behind it. A response such as, "I appreciate your concern, but I've made this decision for my well-being, and I'd prefer to keep these matters between myself and [narcissist's name]," can help assert your boundaries without escalating the situation.

It's also important to maintain your boundaries firmly. This might involve saying something like, "I'm not comfortable discussing this matter any further. Let's focus on other topics," or in more persistent cases, reducing contact with the individual.

Avoid getting drawn into defending yourself or justifying your actions. Remember, the goal is to protect your well-being and maintain the progress you've made in distancing yourself from the narcissist's influence. Engaging in lengthy explanations or debates often serves only to further the narcissist's agenda.

Last, remember the importance of emotional self-care when dealing with flying monkeys. These interactions can be emotionally taxing, so it's important to lean on your support system and engage in self-care practices that help maintain your emotional equilibrium.

Navigating Revenge Seeking

Revenge can come out in different ways: spreading rumors, starting smear campaigns, harassing legally, or confronting directly.

It's important to stay composed and not react impulsively. Revenge-seeking narcissists often thrive on the emotional reactions they provoke, as it gives them a sense of power and control. By responding calmly and not engaging in tit-for-tat retaliation, you deny them this satisfaction. Employing this approach doesn't mean that you are consenting to their behavior; rather, it's a conscious choice to protect your well-being and not fuel their manipulative tactics.

When revenge-seeking behavior starts affecting your reputation, relationships, or legal standing, it's important to document everything. Keep records of any communication, actions, or incidents that could be relevant. This documentation can be vital if legal action becomes necessary or if you need to defend your reputation or actions.

Seeking legal or professional advice is often a prudent step when dealing with more severe forms of revenge-seeking. Legal professionals or counselors specializing in dealing with high-conflict personalities can offer valuable guidance and support. They can also help you navigate the complexities of the situation while ensuring your rights and interests are protected.

It's also important to reinforce your support network during these times. Dealing with revenge-seeking behavior can be stressful and isolating. Friends, family, or support groups can provide emotional support, practical advice, and a sense of perspective. They can remind you that you're not alone in this and help you maintain a sense of normalcy amid the turmoil.

Finally, focus on self-care and maintaining your routine as much as possible. Engaging in activities that promote your well-being, such as exercise, hobbies, or relaxation techniques, can help mitigate the stress associated with dealing with revenge-seeking behavior.

Countering DARVO

When confronted with DARVO, it's important to keep it real and assert yourself.

Start by recognizing the pattern as it unfolds. This awareness is crucial in preventing you from being drawn into the narcissist's distorted narrative. When a narcissist denies their actions, attacks you for confronting them, and then positions themselves as the victim, it's a classic implementation of this tactic.

Maintain a focus on the facts. Make sure to document any relevant interactions and events so you can refer back to them when the narcissist tries to manipulate the truth. For example, if a narcissist denies saying something hurtful and then accuses you of being overly sensitive or aggressive, refer to the documented evidence to reaffirm the truth of the situation.

Communicate your perspective clearly and firmly. If you're being accused or attacked, respond with statements that are based on facts and evidence, rather than emotions. For example, you might say, "I understand you see things differently, but here is what happened…" This approach helps keep the conversation grounded in reality.

Avoid getting entangled in emotional arguments. DARVO is designed to provoke an emotional response and create confusion. By staying calm and not engaging in a heated argument, you reduce the effectiveness of this tactic. This doesn't mean you're accepting the narcissist's perspective, but choosing to respond in a way that preserves your sanity and dignity.

Seeking external support, such as counseling or legal advice, can also be beneficial, especially if the DARVO tactic is causing significant distress or affecting your life substantially. Professional guidance can provide you with strategies to handle the situation and support your mental and emotional health.

The key lies in staying anchored to the truth, communicating assertively, and not allowing the narcissist's manipulation to sway your understanding of the situation.

Dealing With Emotional Blackmail

Emotional blackmail can be subtle or overt, but it always involves using your emotions against you in order to meet the narcissist's needs or demands. The key to dealing with this tactic lies in recognizing it, maintaining emotional distance, and reinforcing your personal boundaries.

First, identify instances of emotional blackmail. The narcissist might guilt trip you, threaten to withdraw affection, or hint at bad things happening if you don't do what they want. For instance, a narcissist may say, "If you truly loved me, you wouldn't think twice about doing this for me," or, "I'll only be satisfied if you do as I say." Acknowledging these statements as emotional coercion is the primary step in combating them.

Once you've identified emotional blackmail, remind yourself of your right to make decisions based on your needs and values, not out of fear, guilt, or obligation imposed by someone else. Affirming your rights internally is crucial in building the resilience needed to resist this form of manipulation.

Setting and communicating clear boundaries is also essential. Let the narcissist know what behavior you find unacceptable and stick to your limits. For instance, if the narcissist tries to guilt-trip you into canceling plans to accommodate their needs, you could respond with, "I understand you're upset, but my plans are important, and I won't cancel them."

It's equally important to not engage in a defensive dialogue. Narcissists thrive on the emotional reactions they can provoke. Responding calmly and not giving in to the drama can often diffuse the situation. Instead of defending your choices, simply state them and refuse to be drawn into an argument.

Last, seek support from friends, family, or a professional. Dealing with emotional blackmail can be draining and confusing. Having a support network provides an external perspective and emotional validation, helping you to stay grounded in your truth.

A Quick Recap

Throughout our exploration, we've uncovered a variety of strategies that empower individuals to effectively handle these challenging dynamics. Let's consolidate these insights into a cohesive recap, emphasizing the key elements of each approach:

1. **Trust and Validation Against Gaslighting:** Keeping a record of events to reaffirm your reality is crucial when countering gaslighting. Trusting your memories and experiences helps maintain a clear sense of truth against the narcissist's distortions.

2. **Objective Response to Guilt Trips:** Recognizing and objectively assessing guilt-tripping tactics enables you to maintain autonomy and communicate your boundaries assertively.

3. **Fact-Based Approach to Projection:** Responding to projection with facts and maintaining emotional detachment helps protect your sense of self and preserves your mental well-being.

4. **Direct Communication in Triangulation:** Addressing triangulation involves direct communication with all parties and avoiding involvement in the narcissist's manipulative plot.

5. **Self-Independence Amid Love Bombing:** Recognizing love bombing and maintaining emotional independence is key to navigating this overwhelming phase without losing perspective.

6. **Integrity in Smear Campaigns:** Maintaining your integrity and openly communicating with your network are vital when facing smear campaigns.

7. **Fact-Centric Approach to Playing the Victim:** Focusing on facts and seeking external validation can help maintain your perspective when a narcissist plays the victim.

8. **Boundary Enforcement in Hoovering:** Standing firm in your boundaries and recalling past patterns are essential when dealing with hoovering attempts.

9. **Assertiveness With Flying Monkeys:** Clear communication and boundary setting are crucial when responding to individuals influenced by the narcissist.

10. **Legal Preparedness for Revenge Seeking:** Seeking legal advice and avoiding direct confrontation are prudent when navigating revenge-seeking behavior.

11. **Clarity in Countering DARVO:** Staying grounded in facts and not getting drawn into the narcissist's distorted narrative is key in countering DARVO tactics.

12. **Emotional Distance From Emotional Blackmail:** Recognizing and maintaining emotional distance helps counter emotional blackmail effectively.

13. **Documenting Interactions:** Keeping records of conversations and communications is essential, especially in situations involving potential legal or workplace issues.

14. **Practicing Detachment:** Emotional detachment allows for more objective and less reactive responses to the narcissist's behavior.

15. **Self-Care Priority:** Engaging in self-care activities strengthens your mental and emotional health, equipping you to handle stressful interactions.

16. **Educational Empowerment:** Understanding narcissism and its behaviors can provide valuable insights for handling these interactions wisely.

These strategies form a comprehensive toolkit for anyone dealing with narcissistic individuals. Remember, the goal isn't to change the narcissist but to empower yourself to handle these interactions with confidence, maintaining your emotional health and personal integrity. With these tools, you're better equipped to navigate the challenges of narcissistic relationships effectively and resiliently.

CHAPTER 7:

It's Your Time to Thrive

Imagine the weight of the dilemma before you: whether to hold onto or break free from a narcissist in your life. What if this person is not just an acquaintance, but your own child or a close family member? The dilemma intensifies. The decision to stay in such a relationship is fraught with complexities and emotional turmoil. It's not just a simple matter of enduring negative behaviors; it's about finding a way to coexist, protect yourself, and possibly even nurture positive change. I dedicate this chapter to unraveling these complexities, providing you with the insight and tools necessary to navigate this challenging terrain. We'll delve into the roles, scenarios, and crucial strategies like bolstering self-esteem and establishing firm boundaries, all tailored for those who choose to stay in these intricate relationships.

Understanding the Dynamics of Staying

A relationship with a narcissist often feels like being cast in a play without a script, where the roles and scenes constantly shift in unexpected ways. Understanding these roles and scenarios is vital for anyone who finds themselves in this complex dynamic, as it offers insights into the narcissist's behavior and how you might be affected.

In these relationships, people unknowingly take on certain roles, each with its own challenges. The enabler, for instance, might justify or rationalize the narcissist's behavior, often at great personal cost. This role can be especially challenging, as it involves a delicate balance between caring for the narcissist and preserving one's own well-being. The enabler's actions, though well-intentioned, might inadvertently perpetuate the toxic cycle, and recognizing this pattern is crucial in starting to break free from it.

The scapegoat, in contrast, is often on the receiving end of the narcissist's negative behavior. They are typically blamed for the narcissist's shortcomings and failures, leading to feelings of marginalization and injustice. Understanding this role is key to countering the unwarranted blame and criticism and to fostering a sense of self-worth that is independent of the narcissist's opinions.

Then there's the golden child, frequently idealized by the narcissist. This role might seem favorable, but it comes with its own set of pressures and unrealistic expectations. The golden child may struggle with their sense of identity, feeling that they must continuously live up to the narcissist's idealized version of them, which can be both exhausting and unsustainable.

The scenarios playing out within these roles can range from subtle manipulations to outright emotional outbursts. A narcissist might employ charm and charisma to mask their more controlling and self-centered tendencies. In other instances, their behavior may be more overt, displaying anger, jealousy, or volatility without provocation. Navigating these scenarios requires a keen understanding of the narcissist's behavior patterns. Recognizing the signs of manipulation or emotional abuse is essential in maintaining your emotional health and sense of self.

For those in a relationship with a narcissist, it's important to remember that these roles are often fluid, and one might move between them based on the narcissist's current needs or state of mind. This realization can be both a challenge and an opportunity: a challenge in its unpredictability and an opportunity because it provides a window into understanding and eventually changing the dynamics of the relationship.

In the following sections, we'll explore strategies to build self-esteem and establish firm boundaries, which are crucial for anyone interacting with a narcissist. These tools are vital in navigating the complex roles and scenarios characteristic of these relationships, helping you maintain a sense of agency and emotional well-being.

The Importance of Self-Esteem

Self-esteem is far more profound than mere self-assurance; your inner compass guides how you perceive and value yourself in the face of adversity. This self-respect and confidence in your own worth are crucial when entangled in the complexities of a relationship with a narcissist.

Self-esteem affects how you see yourself and how you engage with the world. When you're dealing with a narcissist who constantly undermines your self-worth, having strong self-esteem is like having an anchor in a rough sea. This inner strength is vital in lessening the psychological consequences commonly associated with such relationships, like anxiety or depression. The field of positive psychology underscores the importance of self-esteem as a key ingredient for a fulfilling life, emphasizing its role in maintaining mental health and personal well-being (Ackerman, 2019).

Pathways to Rebuilding Self-Esteem

When your self-esteem has been eroded in the wake of narcissistic abuse, professional therapy can be a beacon of light. Strategies such as CBT help rebuild self-esteem. CBT, in particular, focuses on identifying and challenging the negative thought patterns often imposed by a narcissistic partner. By addressing these underlying issues, therapy can play a crucial role in rebuilding a healthy, resilient sense of self-worth.

Meditation and mindfulness practices also emerge as powerful allies in enhancing self-awareness and fostering a compassionate relationship with oneself. These practices, rooted in being present and nonjudgmental about one's experiences, help in creating an emotional buffer against the narcissist's attempts to undermine your self-esteem. They encourage a grounding in the here and now, minimizing the impact of external negativity on your internal sense of value.

Engaging in activities that reinforce your sense of competence and self-achievement is a practical approach to boosting self-esteem. This could involve pursuits that resonate with your passions or skills, serving as a reminder of your capabilities and worth. Surrounding yourself with people who acknowledge and appreciate your true value is equally vital (*Self-Esteem*, 2012). These positive relationships offer a counterbalance to the negative dynamics of a narcissistic relationship, reflecting a more accurate and affirming image of yourself.

The Power of Positive Self-Talk and Self-Compassion

Practicing self-compassion and engaging in positive self-talk are crucial steps in this journey. This involves consciously replacing the narcissist's demeaning narrative with affirmations of your worth and capabilities. It's about retraining your mind to offer yourself the kindness, understanding, and support that you deserve, as outlined in self-help resources and therapy-focused articles.

Developing and upholding self-esteem while in a relationship with a narcissist is a complex and individual process. It involves understanding the critical role of self-esteem, seeking therapeutic support, practicing mindfulness, engaging in empowering activities, and fostering supportive relationships. This comprehensive approach not only helps to fortify your self-esteem against the challenges posed but also empowers you to navigate the relationship with dignity, resilience, and a renewed sense of self.

Navigating Boundaries in Narcissistic Relationships

Understanding and maintaining personal boundaries is crucial when dealing with a narcissist. These boundaries are your emotional, mental, and physical safeguards that help define how you expect to be treated. They are pivotal in maintaining not just your sense of self but your overall well-being.

Boundaries in any relationship, but especially one involving a narcissist, are akin to personal laws or principles that govern how you allow others to interact with you. They protect your personal space, your emotional health, and your mental peace. These boundaries might include your availability for communication, the level of emotional intimacy you're comfortable with, or even the extent to which you share personal information.

For those entangled in relationships with narcissists, who often ignore or trample over personal boundaries, setting and maintaining these limits becomes a critical act of self-preservation. It's about knowing where you draw the line and ensuring this line is respected.

Boundaries are vital for your mental health and emotional well-being. They allow you to express your needs and desires without succumbing to guilt or manipulation (Campbell, 2016). Let's remember that narcissists thrive on breaking down these boundaries to assert control and having firm boundaries in place can be your armor against such invasive tactics. They help prevent you from falling into patterns of codependency and enable you to maintain your individuality, which is crucial for your mental health.

Types of Boundaries

Boundaries come in various forms, each serving a unique purpose in your relationship with a narcissist. Emotional boundaries help you manage your emotional interaction with the narcissist, protecting your feelings and helping you maintain emotional stability. Physical boundaries, which involve your personal space and physical touch, ensure your comfort and safety. Mental boundaries protect your thoughts and opinions, allowing you to maintain your own beliefs and viewpoints in the face of the narcissist's often dominating personality.

In relationships with narcissists, these boundaries provide a framework for interactions that are healthy and respectful. They safeguard against the typical narcissistic tactics of manipulation and control, enabling a more balanced dynamic in the relationship.

Setting Boundaries Effectively

Setting boundaries with a narcissist requires clarity and directness. You need to be clear about what behavior you will not tolerate. This could range from derogatory comments to invasions of privacy. Communicating these boundaries assertively is essential. It's not about confrontation but about standing your ground firmly and respectfully.

Consistency in enforcing these boundaries is key. Narcissists may test these boundaries repeatedly, so maintaining them consistently is crucial. This might mean reiterating your stance multiple times or taking actions to reinforce your boundaries, like stepping back from the situation when your limits are pushed.

Establishing and enforcing boundaries is an ongoing process that requires self-awareness, clarity, and persistence. By understanding the boundaries and their importance, and by learning to set and maintain them effectively, you create a protective barrier for your emotional and mental well-being. This process empowers you to maintain a sense of self in the challenging dynamic of a narcissistic relationship.

When to Walk Away

The decision to walk away is deeply personal and often fraught with emotional complexity. It marks a critical juncture where the preservation of your mental, emotional, and physical well-being takes precedence. This part of the chapter delves into understanding when to make this difficult choice and how to navigate the process effectively.

Knowing when to leave a relationship with a narcissist hinges on recognizing certain telltale signs. It's about closely monitoring the impact the relationship has on your mental, emotional, and physical health. Consistent feelings of mental exhaustion, emotional distress, or a sense of dread about interactions with the narcissist are clear indicators that the relationship may be too detrimental to continue.

Persistent feelings of unhappiness, worthlessness, or fear within the relationship are significant red flags. These feelings often signal that the relationship is not just challenging, but actively harmful. It's crucial to listen to these emotional signals and acknowledge them as valid reasons for considering an exit from the relationship.

Strategizing the Exit

When you decide that leaving the relationship is the best course of action, it's important to approach the situation with a clear plan. This involves mentally and emotionally preparing for the conversation where you express your decision. Being clear and firm about your reasons for leaving can help you stay resolute in the face of potential emotional manipulation or guilt-tripping from the narcissist.

During this time, leaning on a support system is invaluable. Friends, family, or professional counselors can offer the emotional backing and practical advice you need. They can provide a sounding board for your feelings and thoughts, helping you navigate the breakup process with greater clarity and support.

Anticipating and Handling the Reaction

Bracing yourself for the narcissist's response is an essential part of your exit strategy. Their reactions can range widely—from expressions of anger and attempts at guilt-tripping to promises of change. These responses are often tactics aimed at regaining control or prolonging the relationship. It's important to remember that these are typical patterns of behavior for narcissists when faced with the loss of control.

Prioritizing self-care during this period is paramount. Surround yourself with people who understand and support your decision. Engaging in activities that promote your well-being and seeking professional help, if needed, can also be crucial in maintaining your emotional and mental health during this challenging time.

This is not a step taken lightly. It often comes after much contemplation and a realization that the relationship is irreversibly harmful to your well-being. Recognizing the signs that it's time to leave, preparing for the conversation, and bracing for the narcissist's response are crucial steps in this process. By focusing on your well-being, seeking support, and approaching the situation with a clear plan, you can navigate this challenging transition with strength and resilience.

Looking Ahead: Embracing Self-Discovery and Reclaiming Identity

Our in-depth analysis focused on understanding the dynamics of relationships with narcissists, stressing the importance of recognizing and adapting to these roles and scenarios. Central to this discussion has been the emphasis on building and maintaining self-esteem, an essential component for anyone entangled in the web of a narcissistic relationship. We've explored how bolstering your sense of self-worth serves as a shield, protecting you from the adverse psychological impacts these relationships often entail.

Equally important has been our focus on establishing and enforcing boundaries. We've seen how setting these personal rules and limits is crucial in delineating how you wish to be treated, allowing you to maintain your sense of self and emotional well-being even in the most trying circumstances.

The chapter also addressed one of the most challenging aspects of such relationships: recognizing when it's time to walk away. We've covered the signs that indicate a relationship is more harmful than beneficial and provided strategies for ending the relationship while preparing for the potential backlash.

The goal has been to underscore the importance of prioritizing your well-being and mental health, providing you with the tools and knowledge to make informed decisions that are right for you.

As we turn the page to the next chapter called "Know Your Worth," we build upon the concepts discussed here. The focus will shift to self-discovery and reclaiming your identity and self-worth in the aftermath of a narcissistic relationship. This next chapter is about healing, growth, and empowerment. It's about understanding that your value does not diminish because of someone else's inability to see your worth. We'll explore how to rediscover and embrace your true self, finding strength and resilience in the journey ahead.

The path to recovering and rebuilding after such relationships is not just about moving on; it's about moving forward with a renewed sense of self, a deeper understanding of your strengths, and an unshakable belief in your worth.

CHAPTER 8:

Know Your Worth

To be yourself in a world that is constantly trying to make you
something else is the greatest accomplishment.
–Ralph Waldo Emerson

Emerson's words capture the essence of what it means to emerge from
the shadow of narcissistic abuse. They echo the core theme of this
chapter: the often arduous but ultimately fulfilling journey toward
rediscovering and affirming your self-worth. This chapter is a tribute to
your resilience, a guide to help you navigate the path of healing and
self-discovery.

Our journey begins with understanding the complexities of starting
anew after experiencing narcissistic abuse. This path is rarely linear or
simple. It's a journey filled with moments of introspection, obstacles,
and gradual awakenings. We will explore why it's challenging to leave a
narcissist, the lasting effects of such relationships, and the steps for
healing and self-recovery.

As we progress, our focus shifts to the gentle art of rebuilding. Here,
the emphasis lies on the crucial role of self-care in the healing process.
We'll explore the different aspects of self-care and how each
contributes to the rejuvenation of your self-esteem and confidence. I'll
offer you practical, actionable advice on crafting a self-care routine.
This routine isn't just about physical or mental well-being; it's a
nurturing embrace for your soul and a way to strengthen the very core
of your being.

Finally, we touch upon a vital aspect of your healing journey: the power
of seeking help. Whether it's turning to trusted friends and family or

seeking professional therapy, asking for help is a brave and crucial step toward healing. This section is about showing you the value of support.

My goal is to provide you with a compassionate and empowering companion through the trials you've faced in a relationship with a narcissist. This chapter isn't just about recovering from the past; it's about celebrating who you are and embarking on a journey to reclaim your identity filled with confidence and strength. It's about recognizing that, despite everything, your worth is indisputable and unbreakable. Let's walk this path together, toward a future where you stand tall, embracing your true self with all the resilience and grace you possess.

Starting Again: Healing

Narcissistic abuse often disguises itself as something less sinister, making it difficult to detect. This type of abuse is not about overt aggression or physical intimidation; rather, it's a complex blend of emotional manipulation, psychological control, and a pattern of behaviors that systematically undermine the victim's self-esteem and autonomy.

Consider the experience of Ricardo, a dedicated and empathetic individual, who found himself entangled in the manipulative web woven by his partner, Emma. Emma was charismatic and compelling, but beneath her magnetic exterior lay a penchant for manipulation that slowly unfolded as their relationship progressed.

Ricardo initially perceived Emma's intense interest in his life and constant need for attention as signs of love and dedication. However, as time passed, this attention turned into control. Emma began dictating who Ricardo could spend time with, subtly isolating him from friends and family. She would often play the victim, twisting situations to blame Ricardo for her emotional distress, making him perpetually feel like he was walking on eggshells.

One of the most insidious tactics employed by Emma was gaslighting. She would deny events or conversations, making Ricardo question his memory and sanity. This continuous doubt eroded Ricardo's confidence, leaving him dependent on Emma's version of reality.

Another aspect of Emma's narcissistic abuse was her need to maintain a facade of perfection. She projected an image of an ideal relationship to the outside world, while simultaneously demeaning Ricardo in private. This disparity created a confusing dichotomy for Ricardo, making it difficult for him to reconcile the public image with his private turmoil.

Ricardo also faced a barrage of subtle but constant criticisms. Emma's remarks, often framed as jokes or constructive feedback, were designed to belittle him. These comments, coupled with intermittent affection, kept Ricardo in a state of emotional unpredictability, always striving for brief moments of kindness amid the ongoing criticism.

Over time, the cumulative effect of these behaviors began to take a toll on Ricardo. His sense of self-worth diminished, his autonomy eroded, and he found himself constantly striving to meet Emma's ever-changing expectations.

Narcissistic abuse is not always loud or violent; it's the quiet, persistent chipping away at a person's sense of self, often leaving deep emotional scars that take time and effort to heal.

The Lingering Shadows: Long-Term Effects of Narcissistic Abuse

The impact of narcissistic abuse lingers long after the relationship is over. These effects often burrow deep into the psyche of the victim, manifesting in various emotional and psychological challenges.

Take the case of James, who had endured years of narcissistic abuse from his partner, Clara. On the surface, James appeared to have moved on, but beneath the facade, he grappled with enduring emotional turmoil. The relationship with Clara, marked by a cycle of emotional manipulation and control, had left James with deep-seated anxiety and trust issues.

One of the most significant long-term effects James faced was chronic anxiety. This anxiety was not just a fleeting feeling of nervousness; it was a constant companion that colored his every interaction. He found himself second-guessing people's intentions, always on edge, waiting for the other shoe to drop. This state of heightened alertness is a common aftermath of narcissistic abuse, as victims often remain in a prolonged state of psychological hyperarousal, akin to what is seen in PTSD (Cox, 2019).

Depression is another common long-term effect. For James, the joy in life had dimmed. Activities that once brought him happiness now felt empty. He often felt a sense of hopelessness, questioning his worth and doubting whether he would ever truly be free from the impact of the abuse.

James's ability to trust others, especially in intimate relationships, was severely compromised. The constant manipulation and gaslighting by Clara had eroded his ability to trust his judgment and the intentions of others. This mistrust often leads to isolation, as survivors like James withdraw from relationships to protect themselves from potential harm.

Survivors may also experience physical health issues as a result. Stress-related illnesses such as heart disease, gastrointestinal problems, and autoimmune disorders are more common in individuals who have experienced prolonged emotional stress, including narcissistic abuse (Cox, 2019).

Recovery for James, and many others like him, is a slow and challenging process. The long-term effects of narcissistic abuse can't be simply shaken off; they require time, patience, and often professional intervention to heal. This healing journey involves acknowledging the abuse, understanding its impact, and slowly rebuilding trust in oneself and others.

In conclusion, the long-term effects of narcissistic abuse are profound and pervasive, affecting mental, emotional, and physical well-being. Survivors often face a complex journey of recovery. However, with support, understanding, and intervention, there is a path forward to healing and reclaiming a life marked by health, trust, and genuine happiness.

Building Slowly: Rediscovering and Reinforcing Self

When Leo ended his relationship with a narcissistic partner, he found himself adrift in a sea of confusion and self-doubt. The relationship was a roller-coaster of emotions, with love and control mixed together. This had left Leo questioning not **just his worth but the very** essence of who he was. As he stepped away from the relationship, it wasn't just about escaping the toxicity, it was about rediscovering and reclaiming the person he had lost in its midst.

The journey wasn't straightforward. It began with the challenging task of sifting through the remnants of his former self, understanding what was truly his and what had reflected his partner's manipulations. A crucial part of this process was rekindling his love for music, a passion that had been silenced in the whirlwind of his relationship. Returning to his guitar, Leo found in music a familiar friend and a means of expression that words alone couldn't capture. Each note he played was a step toward reclaiming a piece of himself that had been buried.

But the path to healing was more than just reconnecting with old passions; it was also about learning to be kind to himself. Through journaling, Leo began unraveling his thoughts and emotions, confronting the pain and insecurities that had been ingrained in him. He learned the art of self-compassion, recognizing that healing was not a linear journey and that moments of vulnerability were part of the process. It was through these reflective moments that Leo saw himself in a new light: not as the victim of his past, but as the architect of his future.

Rebuilding his social connections was another key aspect of recovery. For so long, his partner's influence had overshadowed his relationships. Reconnecting with friends and family meant relearning how to engage in relationships where his thoughts and feelings were acknowledged and valued. These rekindled relationships provided Leo with a support network that was crucial in his journey to recovery.

Leo's story is not just about the struggles of overcoming narcissistic abuse: It's a testament to the resilience of the human spirit. It's about finding joy in rediscovering oneself and the liberation that comes from breaking free from the chains of manipulation.

Embarking on the healing journey after escaping the grasp of narcissistic abuse is an experience that involves much more than just emotional recovery; it demands a holistic approach to self-care. This vital aspect of the healing process is often overlooked but is essential in rebuilding a sense of self-worth and well-being. For many survivors, the practice of self-care becomes the foundation upon which they reconstruct their lives, cultivating resilience and strength to move forward.

Embracing Self-Care for Holistic Healing

Self-care when recovering from narcissistic abuse encompasses a broad range of practices aimed at nurturing both mental and physical health. One of the most transformative aspects of this journey is the integration of mindfulness and meditation. These practices offer survivors a pathway to mental clarity and inner peace (Raypole, 2020). Mindfulness allows individuals to stay grounded in the present moment, helping to mitigate the lingering effects of past trauma. It becomes a tool for distancing oneself from intrusive thoughts and focusing on personal growth and healing.

Physical exercise also emerges as a crucial element in the self-care regimen. Regular physical activity not only boosts physical health but also contributes significantly to mental well-being. The endorphins released during exercise can counteract feelings of depression and lethargy, which are common in the aftermath of abuse, bringing a sense of vitality and joy.

Nutrition and rest play equally important roles in the healing process. Proper nutrition provides the energy to face daily challenges, while adequate rest is essential for mental and emotional resilience. This approach to self-care is about more than just physical sustenance; it's about nurturing the body to create a conducive environment for recovery.

Beyond individual practices, the concept of social self-care is pivotal. This involves actively seeking and nurturing supportive relationships. For many survivors, reconnecting with friends and family is crucial in combating the isolation experienced during and after the abusive relationship. These relationships provide emotional support, affirmation, and a reminder of one's inherent worth.

The journey of self-care is comprehensive and multidimensional. It's a balanced approach that encompasses both physical health and mental well-being. This process is about affirming one's value and showing oneself the love and respect that were often denied in the abusive relationship. Through such practices, survivors find the strength to continue their journey, thus emerging stronger, more empowered, and ready to rebuild a life marked by self-respect, joy, and fulfillment.

It's a powerful testimony to the importance of taking control of one's health and well-being, serving as a reminder that through dedicated self-care practices, individuals can rediscover their worth and reclaim a life of happiness and self-empowerment.

The Synergy of Reengagement and Support

This journey, vital to reclaiming a sense of self, intertwines the internal process of reengagement with personal interests and the external cultivation of nurturing relationships.

For many survivors, the healing process begins with a return to activities and hobbies that once brought joy and a sense of identity. Narcissistic relationships often overshadow these personal passions, leaving individuals disconnected from their true selves. Rekindling these interests is a powerful act of self-affirmation. It's a statement that one's unique qualities and talents are valuable and deserving of attention. Whether it's picking up a paintbrush after years of neglect, strumming a guitar, immersing in a long-lost hobby, or exploring new pursuits, this reengagement is a celebration of individuality. It serves as a reminder of the person they were before the relationship and who they can be again. Each step in this direction is a step toward rebuilding self-esteem and independence.

Parallel to this journey of self-discovery is the equally important task of building a supportive network. The isolation experienced in a narcissistic relationship can leave deep scars of loneliness and misunderstanding. Reeestablishing connections with friends and family or finding solace in support groups offers much-needed emotional scaffolding. These connections provide not just comfort but also perspective—a reminder that one is not alone in their experiences. They offer a sounding board for thoughts and feelings as well as a safe space for expression and validation. In moments of doubt, these relationships provide strength and encouragement, serving as a crucial counterbalance to the negative narratives ingrained by past abuse.

The interplay between personal reengagement and social support is where true healing flourishes. Indulging in personal interests restores a sense of joy and fulfillment, while supportive relationships offer empathy and understanding. This combination creates a nurturing environment for growth and recovery where individuals can find the strength to overcome the shadows of their past. It's in this space that survivors of narcissistic abuse can slowly piece together their fragmented sense of self, weaving together the threads of their interests, passions, and supportive relationships into a tapestry of renewed identity and self-worth.

This journey, marked by both personal rediscovery and the building of supportive relationships, lays the foundation for a future defined by resilience, self-respect, and fulfillment. It's a testament to the power of embracing one's individuality and the strength found in community, highlighting the importance of both internal growth and external support in overcoming the aftermath of narcissistic abuse.

Embracing Patience and Self-Compassion

When healing, embracing patience and self-compassion emerges as a vital component. This stage of recovery is where survivors learn to extend kindness to themselves, acknowledging that healing is a process that unfolds in its own time.

For those who have endured the complexities of narcissistic relationships, the path to recovery often feels like navigating through a labyrinth of emotions and memories. It requires a deep understanding that healing cannot be rushed. Patience becomes a necessary companion, reminding them that progress is not always linear and that setbacks are part of the journey. This realization shifts the focus to valuing each step of the healing process, regardless of its size.

Simultaneously, self-compassion plays a transformative role in this process. Survivors often battle with self-criticism and guilt, remnants of the manipulative dynamics they've experienced. Self-compassion invites a kinder inner dialogue, one that acknowledges their suffering and offers comfort. It's about replacing the critical voice, often internalized, with a nurturing and understanding one. This shift is not just therapeutic; it's empowering. It allows survivors to view themselves not as victims of their circumstances but as resilient individuals navigating their way to recovery.

To sum up, healing from narcissistic abuse is a journey of self-discovery and personal growth. It involves the challenging task of navigating through the aftermath of abuse, rediscovering and reinforcing self, building a supportive network, and practicing patience and self-compassion. Each of these stages plays a crucial role in helping survivors reclaim their identity and worth.

This journey is a testament to the resilience of the human spirit and the capacity for renewal and transformation. For those who walk this path, it offers not just recovery from past trauma but an opportunity for profound personal growth. The lessons learned, the strength gained, and the self-awareness developed during this journey are invaluable gifts that shape a future filled with hope, self-respect, and fulfillment.

A Beacon in the Dark

Remember that the journey of healing is a road best traveled with the support of others. Recognizing the importance of asking for help marks a significant step in the recovery process. This phase is about acknowledging that one doesn't have to navigate the complexities of healing alone and that seeking support, whether from trusted individuals or professional therapists, can be incredibly beneficial.

Embracing Support From Trusted Individuals

In the intricate journey of healing from narcissistic abuse, embracing support from trusted individuals stands as a beacon of hope and strength. This support, often coming from friends, family, or support groups, plays a critical role in the recovery process. It provides survivors with a haven where they can freely express their feelings and experiences without the fear of judgment or misunderstanding.

For many survivors, the path to healing is laden with feelings of isolation and loneliness. The manipulative nature of narcissistic relationships can sever connections with loved ones, leaving individuals feeling adrift and unsupported. Reaching out to trusted individuals is a courageous step toward breaking this cycle of isolation. It allows survivors to reconnect with the world outside the confines of the abusive relationship.

Just talking to someone who empathizes can be therapeutic in itself. It's an opportunity to be heard and validated, to have one's experiences acknowledged by others who care. These conversations can be a source of immense comfort and reassurance, helping to counter the feelings of worthlessness and self-doubt instilled by the abuser. In these interactions, survivors are reminded of their intrinsic value and the falsehood of the negative narratives they have been made to believe about themselves.

Support from friends and family offers a different perspective: a view of the survivor's situation through the lens of love and care. These perspectives are crucial in reestablishing a survivor's sense of reality, which has often been distorted by the narcissist's manipulation. They help in affirming the survivor's feelings and experiences, reinforcing the belief that the abuse was real and not a product of their imagination.

The strength derived from these connections is immeasurable. It goes beyond mere emotional support; it's about rebuilding the sense of community and belonging that is often lost in abusive relationships. This support network becomes a foundation upon which survivors can reconstruct their lives. It's a reminder that they are not alone in their journey and that there are people who understand and stand by them.

Embracing support is more than just seeking comfort; it's an essential step in the healing process. It's about reconnecting with the world, rebuilding lost relationships, and finding strength in the empathy and understanding of others. This support is invaluable in helping survivors navigate their journey toward recovery, empowering them to reclaim their lives and emerge stronger with a renewed sense of hope and self-worth.

The Role of Professional Therapy

In the relationship's wake, Michael faced a myriad of complex emotions, from confusion and self-doubt to deep-seated pain. The decision to seek therapy emerged from his realization that navigating the path to recovery required more than just time: it needed professional intervention. His therapy sessions became a sanctuary of sorts, a place where he could safely unravel the tangled web of emotions and experiences that had clouded his sense of self. The process was far from easy. It required Michael to confront painful truths and revisit distressing memories. Yet, it was within this challenging environment that he pieced together his fragmented self-esteem and reclaimed his autonomy.

As he worked with his therapist, Michael learned to identify and challenge the negative thought patterns his abuser had instilled in him. They taught him strategies to counteract these harmful beliefs, replacing them with more positive and self-affirming ones. This aspect of his therapy, as discussed in various mental health resources, is critical in addressing the psychological fallout of narcissistic abuse (Simran, 2021). It helps survivors like Michael to reframe their experiences and develop healthier coping mechanisms, ultimately aiding in the reconstruction of their self-worth.

Therapy also provided Michael with the tools to rebuild his confidence. As he progressed, he learned to trust his judgment again, to set boundaries, and to recognize his intrinsic value. The therapeutic journey, though fraught with emotional challenges, became an empowering process that enabled him to break free from the cycle of abuse and manipulation.

Professional guidance is not just a means to recover; it is an integral part of the healing process. It offers a structured and supportive environment where survivors can process their experiences, understand the impact of the abuse, and learn strategies to reclaim their lives. For Michael, as for many others, therapy was the guiding light that led him out of the darkness of abuse, helping him to emerge stronger, more self-aware, and equipped with the tools for a healthier and more empowered future.

The Power of External Support

Embracing external support emerges as a vital pillar. This support, encompassing both personal connections and professional therapy, plays a crucial role in navigating the complexities of healing. It's about understanding that the path to recovery is not one to be walked in solitude but with the guidance and companionship of those who can provide empathy, insight, and understanding.

The first step in embracing this support is recognizing the value of reaching out. For many survivors, this can be a significant hurdle, as narcissistic abuse often instills feelings of isolation and self-doubt. Overcoming this barrier involves acknowledging that seeking help is a courageous step toward healing and self-empowerment. It's about understanding that the insights and empathy provided by others are essential components in the mosaic of recovery.

When turning to friends and family, it's important to choose individuals who offer a safe and nonjudgmental space. These should be people who validate your feelings and experiences, offering comfort and reassurance. Sharing your story with empathetic ears can be incredibly cathartic, helping to dispel the sense of isolation and reaffirming your worth and reality, which may have been distorted by the abuse.

Simultaneously, professional therapy provides a structured and informed approach to healing. A therapist specializing in narcissistic abuse can offer invaluable insights into the dynamics of the abuse and its effects. Therapy sessions become a sanctuary for unburdening the emotional weight carried by survivors. Therapists can guide through the maze of conflicting emotions, helping to unpack and process them in a way that fosters understanding and recovery.

Therapy offers practical tools and strategies for dealing with the aftermath of abuse. From rebuilding self-esteem and trust to learning how to set and enforce healthy boundaries, therapy can equip survivors with the skills needed to navigate their new reality. It's about transforming the lessons learned in therapy into practical steps that can be applied in everyday life.

In embracing external support, it's also crucial to be patient with oneself. Recovery is a journey that unfolds at its own pace, and each step forward, no matter how small, is a stride toward reclaiming control over one's life. The support of friends, family, and therapists acts as a steady hand guiding you through this journey, offering the strength and support needed to overcome the challenges and embrace a future of hope and empowerment.

Embracing external support is a fundamental step in the journey of healing from narcissistic abuse. It's a blend of personal connections and professional guidance that, together, creates a powerful support system. This system offers both comfort and understanding, while equipping us with the essential tools and strategies for a meaningful recovery. As survivors navigate this path, they are reminded of their resilience, their worth, and their ability to rebuild a life defined by self-respect and fulfillment.

Conclusion

As we approach the end of *Dark Psychology and Manipulation,* it is vital to capture the core of what we have uncovered within these pages. This book is more than a guide to recognizing manipulative behaviors; it's a roadmap to personal empowerment in the face of adversity.

The central message we've woven through every chapter is one of awareness and resilience. The understanding that while dark psychology and manipulation are complex and challenging aspects of human relationships, they are not insurmountable. This book has been your companion in uncovering the intricacies of narcissistic tactics, understanding the psychology of manipulators, and, most importantly, learning strategies to safeguard your mental and emotional well-being.

Throughout this journey, we have highlighted the importance of knowledge and self-awareness as tools for empowerment. Recognizing manipulation, establishing boundaries, and reclaiming control over your life are not just abstract concepts but tangible steps toward a healthier, more autonomous existence. The stories and examples shared in these pages, such as those of individuals who have successfully navigated out of the clutches of manipulative relationships, serve as real-life affirmations of the strength and resilience inherent in each of us.

As you move beyond this book, carry with you the understanding that dealing with narcissistic abuse or manipulation is a process—one that is often challenging but immensely rewarding. Consider the stories of those who've walked this path before, who've managed to break free from manipulation and rebuild their lives with a fresh sense of purpose and self-respect. Their journeys underscore the message that while the path may be fraught with challenges, it ultimately leads to a place of greater strength and self-awareness.

I encourage you to share your thoughts on this book. By writing a review, you're not just offering feedback; you're providing guidance and support to others who might navigate similar challenges. Your insights could be the catalyst for someone else's journey toward understanding and overcoming the effects of dark psychology.

I want this book to be a call to action: a prompt to recognize your own strength and resilience in the face of manipulative behaviors. It's an invitation to step out of the shadows of manipulation and into a life where you are the master of your decisions, free from undue influence and emboldened by the knowledge you've gained.

Remember, your journey doesn't end here. It continues each day as you apply these lessons, stand confident in your worth, and embrace a future where you navigate life's complexities with wisdom, courage, and a renewed sense of empowerment.

Glossary

Antisocial Personality Disorder: A condition marked by a long-standing pattern of disregard for other people's rights, often crossing the line and violating those rights.

Bait-And-Switch: A deceptive tactic where a promising offer is replaced with something less desirable after commitment.

Blackmail: The act of coercing someone by threatening to release sensitive or damaging information about them.

Codependency: A psychological condition where an individual exhibits excessive emotional or psychological reliance on a partner, often in a dysfunctional relationship.

Cognitive Dissonance: A state of mental discomfort arising from holding contradictory beliefs, ideas, or values.

Cognitive-Behavioral Therapy (CBT): A form of psychotherapy that aims to change negative thought patterns and behaviors, helping individuals deal with challenges more positively and effectively. It is often used to treat a wide range of disorders, including anxiety, depression, and phobias.

Conduct Disorder: A range of antisocial behaviors in children and adolescents, marked by aggression and a tendency to violate rules and social norms.

Covert Control: Subtle, often unnoticed ways of manipulating or influencing others without their conscious awareness.

Deny, Attack, Reverse Victim, and Offender (DARVO): A manipulative tactic commonly employed by abusers to evade accountability. This strategy involves denying wrongdoing, attacking the accuser, and reversing the roles of victim and offender to deflect blame and maintain control.

Dark Psychology: A study focusing on the underhanded techniques used to unduly influence and control individuals, often at their expense.

Dark Tetrad: Expands the dark triad to include sadism as a fourth trait, highlighting a propensity for cruel and manipulative behaviors.

Dark Triad: A trio of personality traits—narcissism, Machiavellianism, and psychopathy—known for their association with manipulative behavior.

Devaluation: A tactic in abusive dynamics where the abuser systematically undermines the value or worth of their partner.

Dialectical Behavior Therapy (DBT): A type of cognitive-behavioral therapy that focuses on teaching skills in distress tolerance, emotion regulation, mindfulness, and interpersonal effectiveness. DBT is particularly effective in treating personality disorders and chronic patterns of unhealthy behavior.

Emotional Blackmail: The use of emotional manipulation tactics such as fear, obligation, and guilt to control someone's actions.

Flying Monkeys: Individuals who are unwittingly used by a narcissist to execute their bidding, typically involving harassment or targeting of others.

Foot-In-The-Door Technique: A persuasion tactic involving getting a small initial commitment before requesting something larger.

Gaslighting: A disorienting manipulation tactic that causes an individual to doubt their own memory, perception, or sanity.

Guilt-Tripping: A manipulation strategy where guilt is used to influence or control another's actions.

Hoovering: A manipulative strategy often employed by narcissists to lure someone back into a relationship or a certain dynamic.

Love Bombing: Overwhelming someone with excessive affection and attention as a means of manipulation and control.

MacDonald Triad: A set of three behaviors—bedwetting, cruelty to animals, and fire setting—hypothesized as indicators of potential violent tendencies.

Machiavellianism: A personality trait characterized by manipulation, strategic planning, and a focus on personal gain.

Manipulation: The strategic act of swaying someone's thoughts, feelings, or actions for personal gain or advantage.

Mirroring: The act of copying or echoing someone's behavior, expressions, or gestures to establish trust and rapport.

Narcissistic Abuse Cycle: A repetitive pattern in relationships with narcissists, typically involving phases of idealization, devaluation, and discard.

Narcissistic Personality Disorder (NPD): A mental condition marked by an exaggerated sense of self-importance, a deep need for admiration, and a notable lack of empathy.

Personal Boundaries: The limits and rules an individual sets for themselves in relationships to protect their emotional, physical, and mental well-being.

Projection: A defense mechanism where one attributes their own unwanted thoughts or qualities onto others.

Psychopathy: A disorder signified by a lack of empathy, remorse, and often a disregard for moral and social norms.

Revenge Seeking: Pursuing retaliation or payback as a response to perceived wrongs or injustices.

Sadism: The tendency to derive pleasure from causing pain, suffering, or humiliation to others.

Scapegoating: Unfairly blaming an individual or group for problems or issues as a means of diversion or evasion.

Self-Esteem: An individual's internal assessment of their own worth and capabilities.

Silent Treatment: A form of psychological manipulation involving the refusal to communicate or acknowledge someone as a means of control.

Triangulation: A manipulative strategy involving the use of a third party to create instability or tension within a relationship.

Undue Influence: Manipulative tactics exploiting a person's trust, dependency, or vulnerability to alter their decisions or actions.

References

Ackerman, C. (2019, June 19). *What is self-esteem? A psychologist explains*. Positive Psychology. https://positivepsychology.com/self-esteem/

Adler, L. (2020, June 24). *How to deal with someone who's always playing the victim*. Toxic Ties. https://toxicties.com/playing-victim-mentality/

Akin, E. (2021, August 27). *The best way to disarm flying monkeys: 431 survivors' advice*. Unfilteredd. https://unfilteredd.net/how-to-disarm-flying-monkeys/

Akin, E. (2022, June 15). *Why is it so hard to get over a narcissist?* Unfilteredd. https://unfilteredd.net/why-is-it-so-hard-to-get-over-a-narcissist/

Allen, N. (2022, March 13). *This dark personality type is a master manipulator: 6 signs you've met one*. Mindbodygreen. https://www.mindbodygreen.com/articles/machiavellianism

Anderson, N. E., & Kiehl, K. A. (2014). Psychopathy: Developmental perspectives and their implications for treatment. *Restorative Neurology and Neuroscience, 32*(1), 103–117. https://doi.org/10.3233/RNN-139001

Arzt, N. (2023a, May 25). *What is love bombing?* Choosing Therapy. https://www.choosingtherapy.com/love-bombing/

Arzt, N. (2023b, August 18). *15 tips for recovering from narcissistic abuse*. Choosing Therapy. https://www.choosingtherapy.com/recovering-from-narcissistic-abuse/

Benton, E. (2022, May 12). *What is the dark triad?* (J. Johnson, Ed.). PsychCentral. https://psychcentral.com/lib/beware-of-the-dark-triad

BetterHelp Editorial Team. (2023, October 23). *Warning signs of a guilt trip and how to resist it*. Better Help. https://www.betterhelp.com/advice/guilt/warning-signs-of-a-guilt-trip-and-how-to-resist-it/

Booth, S. (2021, June 23). *People with "dark triad" personality traits are manipulative and lack empathy-here's how to steer clear*. Health.

https://www.health.com/condition/antisocial-personality-disorder/dark-triad

Brainwashing. (n.d.). Good Therapy.
https://www.goodtherapy.org/blog/psychpedia/brainwashing

Brainwashing techniques used by alienating parents. (n.d.). PsychLaw.
https://psychlaw.net/brainwashing-techniques-used-by-alienating-parents/

Brennan, D. (2020, November 19). *Manipulation: Symptoms to look for.* WebMD.
https://www.webmd.com/mental-health/signs-manipulation

Brenner, G. (2021, March 21). *A surprising way to reduce dark triad traits.*
Psychology Today.
https://www.psychologytoday.com/us/blog/experimentations/2022
03/a-surprising-way-to-reduce-dark-triad-traits

Burch, K. (2023, December 5). *How to recognize the signs of narcissistic abuse.*
Verywell Health. https://www.verywellhealth.com/narcissistic-abuse-5220194

Caled, D., & Silva, M. J. (2021). Digital media and misinformation: An
outlook on multidisciplinary strategies against manipulation. *Journal of
Computational Social Science, 5.* https://doi.org/10.1007/s42001-021-00118-8

Campbell, L. (2016, May 17). *Personal boundaries: Types and how to set them.*
PsychCentral. https://psychcentral.com/relationships/what-are-personal-boundaries-how-do-i-get-some

Can you have a healthy relationship with a narcissist? (2022, November 8).
Relationships Australia.
https://www.relationshipsnsw.org.au/blog/can-you-have-healthy-relationship-with-narcissist/

Cherry, K. (2019). *The history of narcissistic personality disorder.* Verywell Mind.
https://www.verywellmind.com/the-history-of-narcissistic-personality-disorder-2795569

Cherry, K. (2022, November 7). *What exactly is self-esteem?* Verywell Mind.
https://www.verywellmind.com/what-is-self-esteem-2795868

Cherry, K. (2023, April 4). *What is a guilt trip?* Verywell Mind. https://www.verywellmind.com/what-is-a-guilt-trip-5192249

Cikanavicius, D. (2019, October 20). *Triangulation: The narcissist's best play.* PsychCentral. https://psychcentral.com/blog/psychology-self/2019/10/triangulation-and-narcissism#1

Cikanavicius, D. (2020, February 19). *7 ways narcissists make you feel inferior.* PsychCentral. https://psychcentral.com/blog/psychology-self/2020/02/narcissist-inferior#1

Cooks-Campbell, A. (2021, June 11). *50+ self-care practices and ideas to take better care of yourself.* BetterUp. https://www.betterup.com/blog/self-care-practices

Corelli, C. (2022a, August 29). *Flying monkeys in the world of narcissism: What they are and how to deal with them.* Carla Corelli. https://www.carlacorelli.com/narcissistic-abuse-recovery/flying-monkeys-narcissist/

Corelli, C. (2022b, December 21). *Narcissist triangulation - What it is, why narcissists do it, and how to deal with it.* Carla Corelli. https://www.carlacorelli.com/narcissistic-abuse-recovery/narcissist-triangulation/

Corelli, C. (2023a, January 26). *Narcissistic smear campaign - How to spot it and what to do about it.* Carla Corelli. https://www.carlacorelli.com/narcissism-glossary/narcissistic-smear-campaign/

Corelli, C. (2023b, February 9). *Love bombing: The narcissist's trick to keep you hooked.* Carla Corelli. https://www.carlacorelli.com/narcissistic-abuse-recovery/love-bombing-the-narcissists-trick-to-keep-you-hooked/

Corelli, C. (2023c, February 10). *Narcissist hoovering - How to deal with it.* Carla Corelli. https://www.carlacorelli.com/narcissistic-abuse-recovery/narcissist-hoovering-how-to-deal-with-it/

Cox, J. (2019, October 16). *Narcissistic abuse recovery: Ways to heal.* PsychCentral. https://psychcentral.com/disorders/narcissistic-personality-disorder/narcissistic-abuse-recovery-healing-from-the-discard#effects

Crawford, K. (2023, March 21). *How to spot someone playing victim.* Narcissist Abuse Support. https://narcissistabusesupport.com/how-to-spot-someone-playing-victim/

Cuncic, A. (2022a, April 12). *How does propaganda work?* Verywell Mind. https://www.verywellmind.com/how-does-propaganda-work-5224974

Cuncic, A. (2022b, October 14). *What is triangulation in psychology?* Verywell Mind. https://www.verywellmind.com/what-is-triangulation-in-psychology-5120617

Dexter, G. (2022, February 24). *How to spot manipulative behavior.* Verywell Health. https://www.verywellhealth.com/manipulative-behavior-5214329

Dibdin, E. (2015, May 4). *Narcissistic abuse cycle: Definition, stages, and coping.* PsychCentral. https://psychcentral.com/disorders/the-narcissistic-cycle-of-abuse

The difference between persuasion & manipulation. (2015, April 28). Hoffeld Group. https://www.hoffeldgroup.com/the-difference-between-persuasion-manipulation/

Dolan, E. W. (2021, September 23). Study indicates the dark triad personality traits are more complex than previously thought. *PsyPost.* https://www.psypost.org/2021/09/study-indicates-the-dark-triad-personality-traits-are-more-complex-than-previously-thought-61885

Doll, K. (2019, March 5). *18+ ways to handle emotional blackmail (+ examples & quotes).* Positive Psychology. https://positivepsychology.com/emotional-blackmail/

Dorwart, L. (2023, November 10). *How to tell if someone is a psychopath.* Verywell Health. https://www.verywellhealth.com/psychopath-5235293

Drake, K. (2021, June 4). *How to identify and deal with gaslighting.* PsychCentral. https://psychcentral.com/blog/how-to-identify-and-deal-with-gaslighting

Drescher, A. (2023a, February 22). *Narcissistic love bombing cycle: Idealize, devalue, discard.* Simply Psychology.

https://www.simplypsychology.org/narcissistic-love-bombing-cycle.html

Drescher, A. (2023b, April 2). *Narcissistic hoovering: Signs & how to respond.* Simply Psychology. https://www.simplypsychology.org/narcissistic-hoovering-signs-how-to-respond.html

Drescher, A. (2023d, November 2). *What is narcissistic projection & how to respond.* Simply Psychology. https://www.simplypsychology.org/narcissistic-projection.html

Durham, S., & Young, K. (2023, January 10). *Understanding abuse: Types of gaslighting.* SACAP. https://www.sacap.edu.za/blog/applied-psychology/types-of-gaslighting/

Eatough, E. (2021, October 6). *Why you need a self-care plan (and 5 ways to get started).* BetterUp. https://www.betterup.com/blog/self-care-plan

The Editors. (2023, July 3). *From denial to gaslighting: Decoding DARVO in toxic relationships.* Narcissistic Abuse Rehab. https://www.narcissisticabuserehab.com/from-denial-to-gaslighting-decoding-darvo-in-toxic-relationships/

8 tips for dealing with a narcissist. (2021, December 8). Anchor Therapy. https://www.anchortherapy.org/blog/8-tips-for-dealing-with-a-narcissist-nj-nyc

England, A. (2023, July 14). *What "flying monkeys" mean when we talk about narcissism.* Verywell Mind. https://www.verywellmind.com/narcissists-and-flying-monkeys-7552473

Estee. (2023, May 12). *DARVO: What it is & how to deal with it.* Hopeful Panda. https://hopefulpanda.com/darvo/

Firestone, L. (2019, January 17). *What really goes on in the mind of a narcissist?* PsychAlive. https://www.psychalive.org/what-really-goes-on-in-the-mind-of-a-narcissist/

Firestone, L. (2022, January 19). *Why is it so hard to leave a narcissist?* Psychology Today. https://www.psychologytoday.com/intl/blog/compassion-matters/202201/why-is-it-so-hard-leave-narcissist

Fjelstad, M. (2017a, June 22). *8 things to expect when you break up with a narcissist (A relationship specialist explains)*. Mindbodygreen. https://www.mindbodygreen.com/articles/what-to-expect-when-you-break-up-with-a-narcissist

Fjelstad, M. (2017b, September 5). *15 signs you're dealing with a narcissist*. Mindbodygreen. https://www.mindbodygreen.com/articles/14-signs-of-narcissism

Fleming, L. (n.d.). *How narcissists use DARVO to avoid accountability*. Verywell Mind. https://www.verywellmind.com/protecting-yourself-from-darvo-abusive-behavior-7562730

Frothingham, M. B. (2023, August 31). *Dark triad personality traits*. Simply Psychology. https://www.simplypsychology.org/dark-triad-personality.html

Gaba, S. (2021, May 17). *Spotting the hoovering techniques of a narcissist*. Psychology Today. https://www.psychologytoday.com/intl/blog/addiction-and-recovery/202105/spotting-the-hoovering-techniques-narcissist

Gillette, H. (2022, November 1). *Financial abuse: How to recognize it and tips to cope*. PsychCentral. https://psychcentral.com/health/financial-abuse

Gillis, K. (2022, November 10). *9 narcissistic manipulation tactics & how to deal*. Choosing Therapy. https://www.choosingtherapy.com/narcissistic-manipulation-tactics/

Gillis, K. (2023, March 28). *3 tips to protect yourself from a narcissist's "flying monkeys."* Psychology Today. https://www.psychologytoday.com/intl/blog/invisible-bruises/202303/3-tips-to-protect-yourself-from-a-narcissists-flying-monkeys

Gordon, S. (2020, May 6). *Financial abuse: Often the first sign of domestic abuse*. Verywell Mind. https://www.verywellmind.com/financial-abuse-4155224

Gordon, S. (2022, January 5). *Understanding the manipulative behaviors toxic people use to control*. Verywell Mind. https://www.verywellmind.com/is-someone-gaslighting-you-4147470

Grohol, J. M., & Marie, S. (2021, September 28). *Conduct disorder symptoms.* PsychCentral. https://psychcentral.com/disorders/conduct-disorder-symptoms

Grohol, J. M., & Telloian, C. (2021, March 2). *What are symptoms of antisocial personality disorder?* PsychCentral. https://psychcentral.com/disorders/antisocial-personality-disorder/symptoms

Gupta, S. (2022, August 15). *What is the narcissistic abuse cycle?* Verywell Mind. https://www.verywellmind.com/narcissistic-abuse-cycle-stages-impact-and-coping-6363187

Hall, J. L. (2023, May 5). *The narcissist's airtight victim narrative.* Psychology Today. https://www.psychologytoday.com/intl/blog/the-narcissist-in-your-life/202303/the-narcissists-airtight-victim-narrative

Hammond, C. (2015, November 13). *The dark tetrad: Possibly THE scariest boss.* PsychCentral. https://psychcentral.com/pro/exhausted-woman/2015/11/the-dark-tetrad-possibly-the-scariest-boss#1

Hammond, C. (2017, March 16). *5 ways narcissists smear others.* PsychCentral. https://psychcentral.com/pro/exhausted-woman/2017/03/5-ways-narcissists-smear-others#1

Hartley, D. (2017, November 2). *Machiavellians: Self-made or born that way?* Psychology Today. https://www.psychologytoday.com/us/blog/machiavellians-gulling-the-rubes/201711/machiavellians-self-made-or-born-that-way

Heym, N., & Sumich, A. (2022, April 4). *Psychologists explain the hidden danger of "dark empaths."* PsyPost. https://www.psypost.org/2022/04/psychologists-explain-the-hidden-danger-of-dark-empaths-62846

Himani. (2022, June 22). *Leaving a narcissist: 11 tips and how to move on.* Mantra Care. https://mantracare.org/therapy/narcissistic/leaving-narcissist/

Holland, K. (2018, February 13). *How to recognize the signs of emotional manipulation and what to do.* Healthline. https://www.healthline.com/health/mental-health/emotional-manipulation

Holland, M. (2023, May 17). *Narcissistic triangulation: Definition, examples, & how to respond*. Choosing Therapy. https://www.choosingtherapy.com/narcissistic-triangulation/

Huizen, J. (2020, July 14). *What is gaslighting? Examples and how to respond*. Medical News Today. https://www.medicalnewstoday.com/articles/gaslighting

Is there manipulation in your marriage? (2020). Verywell Mind. https://www.verywellmind.com/manipulation-in-marriage-2302245

Jack, C. (2020, October 7). *Are you a narcissist's flying monkey?* Psychology Today. https://www.psychologytoday.com/intl/blog/women-autism-spectrum-disorder/202010/are-you-narcissist-s-flying-monkey

Jansen, M. (2020, November 23). *Is this how narcissists think?* Psychology Today. https://www.psychologytoday.com/intl/blog/victim-victor/202011/is-how-narcissists-think

Jewell, T. (2020, March 24). *The MacDonald triad: Can 3 behaviors predict a serial killer?* Healthline. https://www.healthline.com/health/macdonald-triad

Joel. (2022, May 11). *Dark psychology: The essential guide to master manipulators*. Bloomsoup. https://bloomsoup.com/dark-psychology/

Jordan, K. (2023, September 5). *Breaking up with a narcissist: 5 tips & what to expect*. Choosing Therapy. https://www.choosingtherapy.com/breaking-up-with-a-narcissist/

Katie M. (2023). *What is a narcissist smear campaign? - Understand this tactic*. Wengood. https://www.wengood.com/en/psychology/stress/art-narcissist-smear-campaign

Kim, J. (2023, June 16). *Tell me all I need to know about narcissistic personality disorder*. Psycom. https://www.psycom.net/personality-disorders/narcissistic

Kristenson, S. (2023a, May 24). *20 manipulation tactics used by gaslighters, narcissists & sociopaths*. Happier Human. https://www.happierhuman.com/manipulation-tactics-wa1/

Kristenson, S. (2023b, August 14). *Narcissistic triangulation: Examples & how to stop it.* Happier Human. https://www.happierhuman.com/narcissistic-triangulation-wa1/

Kritz, F., & Gillihan, S. (2022, December 20). *What is narcissism? Symptoms, causes, diagnosis, treatment, and prevention.* Everyday Health. https://www.everydayhealth.com/narcissism/

Lamothe, C. (2019, December 17). *12 signs you're being hoovered by a narcissist.* Healthline. https://www.healthline.com/health/hoovering

Lancer, D. (2019a). *How to confront narcissists' lethal weapon: Projection.* Psychology Today. https://www.psychologytoday.com/us/blog/toxic-relationships/201903/how-confront-narcissists-lethal-weapon-projection

Lancer, D. (2019b, May 5). *Why narcissists act the way they do.* PsychCentral. https://psychcentral.com/lib/why-narcissists-act-the-way-they-do#1

Lawler, M. (2023, March 17). *What is self-care and why is it critical for your health?* Everyday Health. https://www.everydayhealth.com/self-care/

Lebow, H. (2022, September 21). *How to spot a manipulative person.* PsychCentral. https://psychcentral.com/lib/how-to-spot-manipulation

LeClair, C. (2023, February 5). *Communicating boundaries.* LinkedIn. https://www.linkedin.com/pulse/communicating-boundaries-cassandra-leclair-ph-d-/

Liden, D. (2023, June 12). *What is the connection between narcissism and revenge?* The Health Board. https://www.thehealthboard.com/what-is-the-connection-between-narcissism-and-revenge.htm

Lindberg, S. (2018, September 14). *It's not me, it's you: Projection explained in human terms.* Healthline. https://www.healthline.com/health/projection-psychology

Mancao, A. (2021, April 16). *What do you say when someone's gaslighting you? A therapist's go-to comebacks.* Mindbodygreen. https://www.mindbodygreen.com/articles/how-to-deal-with-gaslighting

Manipulation. (2013, April 16). Good Therapy. https://www.goodtherapy.org/blog/psychpedia/manipulation

Marie, S. (2021, July 26). *Machiavellianism personality traits*. PsychCentral. https://psychcentral.com/lib/machiavellianism-cognition-and-emotion-understanding-how-the-machiavellian-thinks-feels-and-thrives

Marie, S. (2022, April 27). *The guilt trip: How to deal with this manipulation*. PsychCentral. https://psychcentral.com/health/guilt-trip

Martin, S. (2020, April 23). *7 types of boundaries you may need*. PsychCentral. https://psychcentral.com/blog/imperfect/2020/04/7-types-of-boundaries-you-may-need

Mayer, B. A. (2023, June 26). *11 narcissistic manipulation tactics, according to experts*. Parade. https://parade.com/living/narcissistic-manipulation-tactics-according-to-therapists

McBride, K. (2017, May 22). *How does a narcissist think?* Psychology Today. https://www.psychologytoday.com/intl/blog/the-legacy-distorted-love/201705/how-does-narcissist-think

Miller, C. (2021, April 1). *Love bombing – The narcissistic abuse cycle*. The Better You Institute. https://thebetteryouinstitute.com/2021/04/01/love-bombing-the-narcissistic-abuse-cycle/

Mind Tools Content Team. (n.d.). *Understanding the Dark Triad*. Mind Tools. https://www.mindtools.com/au5148p/understanding-the-dark-triad

Mrkonjić, E. (2022, April 28). *What is dark psychology? A 2022 overview*. SeedScientific. https://seedscientific.com/psychology/what-is-dark-psychology/

A narcissist's flying monkeys + 3 tactics to disarm them. (2021, August 16). Abuse Warrior. https://abusewarrior.com/abuse/a-narcissists-flying-monkeys/

Nash, J. (2018, January 5). *How to set healthy boundaries & build positive relationships*. Positive Psychology. https://positivepsychology.com/great-self-care-setting-healthy-boundaries/

National Domestic Violence Hotline. (n.d.). *What is gaslighting?* https://www.thehotline.org/resources/what-is-gaslighting/

Neuharth, D. (2017, April 11). *11 things NOT to do with narcissists*. Psych Central. https://psychcentral.com/blog/narcissism-decoded/2017/04/11-things-not-to-do-with-narcissists#1

Neuharth, D. (2019, July 16). *10 things not to do with narcissists*. Psychology Today. https://www.psychologytoday.com/us/blog/narcissism-demystified/201907/10-things-not-to-do-with-narcissists

Nguyen, J. (2021, September 18). *Getting this kind of text from your ex is a big red flag*. Mindbodygreen. https://www.mindbodygreen.com/articles/hoovering-in-relationships

Ni, P. (2017). *7 stages of gaslighting in a relationship*. Psychology Today. https://www.psychologytoday.com/us/blog/communication-success/201704/7-stages-gaslighting-in-relationship

Nomina. (2022, September 11). *The psychology of a catfisher*. LinkedIn. https://www.linkedin.com/pulse/psychology-catfisher-nomina-wellness/

107 highly empowering quotes to boost your self-worth. (2021, May 11). Gratitude. https://blog.gratefulness.me/20-great-quotes-to-boost-your-self-worth/

Pace, R. (2019, February 8). *How to leave a narcissist: 10 proven ways*. Marriage Advice. https://www.marriage.com/advice/mental-health/leave-a-narcissist/

Pagels, C. (2022, September 8). *How to respond to a guilt trip*. Mindpath Health. https://www.mindpath.com/resource/how-to-respond-to-a-guilt-trip/

Paglia, M. (2021, April 9). *Psychology of trolling: Why people troll online?* The International Psychology Clinic. https://theinternationalpsychologyclinic.com/psychology-of-trolling-why-people-troll-online/

Paler, J. (2019, December 6). *The toxic cycle of emotional blackmail and 7 ways to stop it*. Hack Spirit. https://hackspirit.com/emotional-blackmail/

Parvez, H. (2022, November 18). *List of emotional manipulation tactics.* PsychMechanics. https://www.psychmechanics.com/list-of-emotional-manipulation-tactics/

Patricia. (2021, April 4). *6 stages of emotional blackmail from narcissists.* Inner Toxic Relief. https://innertoxicrelief.com/stages-of-emotional-blackmail/

Patterson, E. (2022, June 1). *DARVO: Deny, attack, reverse victim & offender.* Choosing Therapy. https://www.choosingtherapy.com/darvo/

Peisley, T. (2017, March 14). *Is narcissism common? The answer may surprise you.* SANE. https://www.sane.org/information-and-resources/the-sane-blog/mental-illness/is-narcissism-common-the-answer-may-surprise-you

Peterson, T. J. (2023, November 3). *Projection: Definition, examples, & use as a defense mechanism.* Choosing Therapy. https://www.choosingtherapy.com/projection/

Psychology Today Staff. (2010). *Dark Triad.* Psychology Today. https://www.psychologytoday.com/us/basics/dark-triad

Psychology Today Staff. (2020). *Projection.* Psychology Today. https://www.psychologytoday.com/us/basics/projection

Raypole, C. (2020, March 30). *Recovery from narcissistic abuse is possible — Here's how.* Healthline. https://www.healthline.com/health/mental-health/9-tips-for-narcissistic-abuse-recovery

Raypole, C. (2020a, March 5). *Emotional blackmail: Definition, how it works, and more.* Healthline. https://www.healthline.com/health/emotional-blackmail

Raypole, C. (2020b, June 25). *8 ways to deal with gaslighting.* Healthline. https://www.healthline.com/health/how-to-deal-with-gaslighting

Raypole, C. (2020c, July 22). *How to spot and respond to a guilt trip.* Healthline. https://www.healthline.com/health/relationships/guilt-trip

Raypole, C. (2021, February 26). *Narcissistic triangulation: Definition, examples, how to respond.* Healthline. https://www.healthline.com/health/narcissistic-triangulation

Regan, S. (2021, December 12). *How exactly to respond when a toxic person tries to guilt trip you*. Mindbodygreen. https://www.mindbodygreen.com/articles/guilt-trips

Reid, S. (2023, March 1). *Setting healthy boundaries in relationships*. Help Guide. https://www.helpguide.org/articles/relationships-communication/setting-healthy-boundaries-in-relationships.htm

Rosbach, M. (2020, July 22). *Narcissists don't learn from their mistakes because they don't think they make any, study shows*. Life at OSU. https://today.oregonstate.edu/news/narcissists-don%E2%80%99t-learn-their-mistakes-because-they-don%E2%80%99t-think-they-make-any-study-shows

Roy, J. (n.d.). *Boundaries: Definition, examples & how to set them*. The Berkeley Well-Being Institute. https://www.berkeleywellbeing.com/boundaries.html

Roy, S. (2022, November 28). *How to respond to a narcissist hoovering you back to them?* The Happiness Blog. https://happyproject.in/respond-narcissist-hoovering/

Sadistic personality disorder: Definition, causes, types, and interventions. (2022, December 12). Counseling Now. https://counselingnow.com/sadistic-personality-disorder/

Sam N. (2023, June 21). *What is dark psychology? Definition of dark psychology (psychology dictionary)*. Psychology Dictionary. https://psychologydictionary.org/dark-psychology/

Sarkis, S. A. (2022, September 25). *7 facts to know about narcissistic "hoovering."* Psychology Today. https://www.psychologytoday.com/intl/blog/here-there-and-everywhere/202209/7-facts-know-about-narcissistic-hoovering

Saxena, S. (2021, November 18). *What is a narcissistic abuse cycle & how does it work?* Choosing Therapy. https://www.choosingtherapy.com/narcissistic-abuse-cycle/

Schwartz, A. (2013, May 17). *Sadistic personality disorder: The Cleveland tragedy*. MentalHelp.Net. https://www.mentalhelp.net/blogs/sadistic-personality-disorder-the-cleveland-tragedy/

Scott, E. (2020). *5 self-care practices for every area of your life*. Verywell Mind. https://www.verywellmind.com/self-care-strategies-overall-stress-reduction-3144729

Self-esteem. (2012). Better Health Channel. https://www.betterhealth.vic.gov.au/health/healthyliving/self-esteem

Self-esteem and mental health. (2019, February 17). Health Direct. https://www.healthdirect.gov.au/self-esteem

Silva Casabianca, S., & Pedersen, T. (2019, March 4). *6 games people with narcissistic personality play*. PsychCentral. https://psychcentral.com/blog/manipulation-games-narcissists-play#takeaway

Simran. (2021, December 27). *Victim narcissist: Types, signs, reasons, treatment, dealing*. Mantra Care. https://mantracare.org/therapy/narcissistic/victim-narcissist/

Smith, M., & Robinson, L. (2019, March 21). *Narcissistic personality disorder*. HelpGuide. https://www.helpguide.org/articles/mental-disorders/narcissistic-personality-disorder.htm

Smith, S. (2018, October 16). *What revenge tactics you can expect from a narcissist*. Marriage.com. https://www.marriage.com/advice/mental-health/revenge-tactics-of-a-narcissist/

Social engineering attack: Hack to manipulate psychology. (2020, February 29). Threat Cop. https://threatcop.com/blog/social-engineering-attack/

Stines, S. (2017a, March 1). *How to stay with a narcissist*. PsychCentral. https://psychcentral.com/pro/recovery-expert/2017/03/how-to-stay-with-a-narcissist#1

Stines, S. (2017b, September 20). *Leaving a person with narcissism: Here comes the smear campaign*. GoodTherapy. https://www.goodtherapy.org/blog/leaving-person-with-narcissism-here-comes-smear-campaign-0920174

The story of Echo and Narcissus. (n.d.). Arlington Classics Academy. https://www.acaedu.net/cms/lib3/TX01001550/Centricity/Domai

n/562/Week%2022%20-
%20The%20Story%20of%20Echo%20and%20Narcissus.pdf

3 empowering ways to respond to a guilt trip. (2022, June 18). Hailey Magee.
https://www.haileymagee.com/blog/2022/6/18/3-empowered-
ways-to-respond-to-a-guilt-trip

Triangulation. (2016, January 8). GoodTherapy.
https://www.goodtherapy.org/blog/psychpedia/triangulation

*Unveiling the depths of dark psychology: A comprehensive exploration of manipulation and
mind control.* (2020, October 27). Sintelly.
https://sintelly.com/articles/dark-psychology-manipulation-and-
mind-control/

Vogel, K., & Craft, C. (2022, April 15). *7 manipulation tactics to know.*
PsychCentral. https://psychcentral.com/lib/tactics-manipulators-
use-to-win-and-confuse-you#stages-of-manipulation

Wakefield, M. (2022, March 12). *Types of flying monkeys: The 2 main kinds of
narcissistic enablers.* Narcissistic Abuse Rehab.
https://www.narcissisticabuserehab.com/types-of-flying-monkeys/

What causes psychopathy. (2021). Psychopathy Is.
https://psychopathyis.org/what-causes-psychopathy/

*What is emotional blackmail? Warning signs, examples, and turning it into something
healthy.* (2023, January 23). Kentucky Counseling Center.
https://kentuckycounselingcenter.com/emotional-blackmail/

Wood, S. (2021, September 6). *Catfishing explained.* Psychology Today.
https://www.psychologytoday.com/intl/blog/the-fraud-
crisis/202108/catfishing-explained

Made in the USA
Las Vegas, NV
04 March 2025

19072428R00085